MW00330378

Economics, Philosophy, and Physics

Economics, Philosophy, and Physics

Ching-Yao Hsieh
Meng-Hua Ye

M. E. Sharpe
Armonk, New York
London, England

Copyright © 1991 by M. E. Sharpe, Inc.
80 Business Park Drive, Armonk, New York 10504

All rights reserved. No part of this book may be reproduced in any
form without written permission from the publisher.

Available in the United Kingdom and Europe from M. E. Sharpe, Publishers,
3 Henrietta Street, London WC2E 8LU.

Library of Congress Cataloging-in-Publication Data

Hsieh, Ching-Yao, 1917–
Economics, philosophy, and physics / Ching-Yao Hsieh and Meng-Hua Ye.
p.   cm.
ISBN 0-87332-759-4.—ISBN 0-87332-760-8 (pbk.)
1. Economics. 2. Philosophy. 3. Physics.
I. Ye, Meng-Hua. II. Title.
HB72.H75   1991
330—dc20
90-19138
CIP

Printed in the United States of America

The paper used in this publication
meets the minimum requirements
of American National Standard
for Information Sciences—Permanence of Paper
for Printed Library Materials, ANSI Z 39.48-1984.

BB   10   9   8   7   6   5   4   3   2   1

To

Robert and Molly Hsieh

Contents

List of Figures

Acknowledgments

We wish to express our thanks to our colleagues at the George Washington University, Professors Bryan L. Boulier, Robert S. Goldfarb, John E. Kwoka, Charles T. Stewart, Anthony M. Yezer, Arjo Klamer, and Richard H. Schlagel, for reading parts of the manuscript and for their valuable comments. Any deficiencies in this book are entirely our own.

Jennifer Lin, Eva Skryjova, and Shonda Davis deserve special thanks for their generous assistance in the preparation of the manuscript.

We also wish to express our appreciation to Bantam Books (for excerpts from *Order out of Chaos* by Ilya Prigogine and Isabelle Stengers, copyright © 1984 by Ilya Prigogine and Isabelle Stengers. Foreword copyright © 1984 by Alvin Toffler. Used by permission of Bantam Books, a division of Bantam, Doubleday, Dell Publishing Group, Inc.; and excerpts from *From Socrates to Sartre: The Philosophic Quest* by T.Z. Lavine, copyright © 1985. Used by permission of Bantam Books, a division of Bantam, Doubleday, Dell Publishing Group, Inc.), Simon & Schuster, Inc., Routledge and Kegan Paul, Inc. (for excerpts from *Wholeness and Implicate Order* by David Bohm, © 1983. Used by permission of Routledge and Kegan Paul, Inc.), W.H. Freeman and Company, and Dr. Benoit B. Mandelbrot for granting permissions to include some quotations from their publications in this book.

Finally, we would like to thank the editors at M.E. Sharpe, Inc., Dr. Richard D. Bartel, Ms. Angela Piliouras, and Ms. Bessie Blum, for their valuable suggestions and superb editing of the text.

Introduction

This book is written for students of economics who would like to know the philosophical underpinnings and scientific foundations of contemporary economic models. With a view of gaining a better perspective of the discipline, economics majors should recognize the important interrelationship between economics, philosophy, and science. Our daily approaches to economic, political, and other social problems are based on philosophy (such as, the world according to *conservatives*, or, the world according to *Marxists*). "The Philosophy of any period," as pointed out by Sir James Jeans, "is always largely interwoven with the science of the period, so that any fundamental change in science must produce reactions in philosophy."[1] It follows that any change in philosophy must influence economics and other social sciences.

The title of this book is *Economics, Philosophy, and Physics*. We have singled out physics among the natural sciences because physics is an all-encompassing discipline. In the words of Paul Davies, "Through physics, all parts of the cosmos from the elementary particles within atoms to the largest astronomical structures can be incorporated into a single conceptual framework."[2]

The basic indivisibility of economics, philosophy, and physics has been demonstrated by a succession of world views through history. As an introduction to this book, we shall begin by considering briefly the classical Greek and the scholastic world views.

The Classical Greek World View

In a world of uncertainty and risks, man has since the beginning of history embarked on the quest for certainty. Even in our time, as Paul Davidson observes, the existence of uncertainty in monetary economy has led man to develop certain uncertainty-reducing institutions such as money and contracts.[3] In the classical Greek era, the philosophers' quest to certainty was demonstrated by their attempts to rationalize nature. John Dewey observed: "If one looks at the foundations of the philosophies of Plato and Aristotle . . . it is clear that the philosophies were systematization in rational form of the content of Greek religious and artistic beliefs. The systematization involved a purification."[4] In other words, the mission of philosophy of Plato and Aristotle was to discover true and certain knowledge. "In this task," write Philip J. Davis and Reuben Hersh, "mathematics had a central place, for mathematical knowledge was the outstanding example of knowledge independent of sense experience, knowledge of eternal and necessary truth."[5]

The center of Greek mathematics was Euclidean geometry, which remained unchallenged up to the middle or late nineteenth century. Davis and Hersh referred to this phenomenon as the "Euclidean Myth" and observe: "It has been the major support for metaphysics, that is, for philosophy which sought to establish some a priori certainty about the nature of the universe."[6]

There were no inner conflicts in classical Greek culture. Morris Kline points out: "Geometry, philosophy, logic and art were all expressions of one type of mind, one outlook on the universe."[7] If one prefers a tinge of mysticism, the soul of the classical Greek culture was designated by Oswald Spengler as "Apollinian": "Apollinian are: mechanical statics, the sensuous cult of the Olympian gods, the politically individual city-state of

Greece, the doom of Oedipus and phallus-symbol.''[8]

The static closure and finiteness of Euclidean geometry are not only reflected in the dominant characteristics of Greek architecture (such as the Greek temple), statues, and paintings, but are also manifested in their approaches to philosophy, science, and economic and other social problems.

Philosophy

Both Plato and Aristotle pictured the universe as an organism. Each part of the universe had its proper place and function: in the words of David Bohm, ''Its activity was seen as an effort to move toward that proper place and to carry out its appropriate function.''[9] Hence, at the core of the Aristotelian philosophy was teleology. The notion of causality associated with the teleological processes was the doctrine of the four causes, namely, Material, Efficient, Formal, and Final causes. It is this doctrine that enabled Aristotle to bridge the dichotomy of the Platonic ''world of ideas'' and the ''world of senses.'' Neither Plato nor Aristotle mentioned explicitly the notion of ''natural law.'' The notion, however, was implicit in their writings. Their approach to everything is holistic, because they treat different systems as a whole.

Science

Aristotle's approach to science focuses on the question ''why?'' There was no inner conflict between his physics and metaphysics. According to Stephen W. Hawking, ''The Aristotelian tradition . . . held that one could work out all the laws that govern the universe by pure thought: it was not necessary to check by observation. So no one until Galileo bothered to see whether bodies of different weight did in fact fall at different speeds.''[10]

Aristotle asserted that all the matters in the universe were made up of four basic elements, namely, earth, air, fire, and water, which were acted upon by two forces, gravity and levity. To Aristotle, the earth was the stationary center of the universe.

The sun, moon, stars, and other planets moved in circular orbits about the earth. The Aristotelian cosmology was subsequently elaborated by Ptolemy in the second century A.D. into a complete geocentric cosmological model.

With regard to the important question of time, Hawking observes: "Both Aristotle and Newton believed in absolute time. That is, they believed that one could unambiguously measure the interval of time between two events, and that this time would be the same whoever measured it, provided they use a good clock. Time was completely separated from and independent of space."[11]

Throughout history every dominating paradigm has been confronted with dissenting views. The Aristotelian paradigm was no exception. As Paul Davies points out:

> In direct opposition to Aristotle were the Greek atomists, such as Demorcitus, who taught that the world is nothing but atoms moving in a void. . . . To the atomists, the universe is a machine in which each component atom moves entirely under the action of the blind forces produced by its neighbors. According to this scheme there are no final causes, no overall plan or end-state towards which things evolve. . . . There was thus already present in ancient Greece the deep conflict between holism and reductionism which persists to this day.[12]

It is ironic that with the advances of Relativity, Quantum, and Chaos theories in our time, we have witnessed the revival of the synthetic and holistic approach.[13]

Economics

The focal points of the economic writings of Plato and Aristotle were community, self-sufficiency, and justice. Whenever they touched on a question of the economy, both Plato and Aristotle adopted the holistic approach: that is, they related all such questions to the totality of society. The role of economic activity, Plato and Aristotle believed, was to facilitate the realization of the well-being of the citizens of the ideal city-state, of a just and harmonious community. To Plato and Aristotle, the economic system was a subset of the Polis.[14] Whereas in the modern market economy, Karl Polanyi points out that, "instead of the economic system being embedded in the social relationships, these relationships are now embedded in the economic system. . . . It was almost impossible to avoid the erroneous conclusion that as 'economic' man was 'real' man, so that economic system was 'real' society."[15]

Technological progress, economic growth, capital accumulation, maximization of individual utility, competitive market mechanism, and efficiency in production, distribution, and consumption were not within their purview. Political stability was considered to be essential to attain the ideal of a just society. There are some differences between the views of Plato and those of Aristotle. For example, Plato believed that the ideal of the "philosopher king" and communism for the rulers and the defenders of the Polis were the best political solutions, whereas Aristotle was in favor of the "rule of law" and constitutional monarchy. However, the Aristotelian economic preconditions of political stability were not so much different from those of Aristotle's teacher.

The indivisibility of economics, philosophy, and physics is also manifested in the Aristotelian version of the "just price." Consistent with his view that one could work out all the laws governing the universe by pure thought, Aristotle's approach to price formation (like Plato before him) was essentially ethical and normative. Polanyi observes: "The postulate of self-sufficiency implied that such trade as was required to restore autarchy was *natural* and, therefore, right."[16] The price compatible with the "natural trade," according to Aristotle, was based on commutative justice, which entailed that when a transaction took place, equivalent values must be exchanged. What constituted equivalence was not in the end very concretely specified, even though it apparently was taken for granted that each participant in a "just" transaction would be rewarded in accordance with his merit or performance as indicated in the distribution of income.

It should be noted that there are a few sprinkles of pure economics in the normative theories of Plato and Aristotle. In the view of Joseph A. Schumpeter, Plato was the sponsor of the antimetallist tradition of monetary theory, because Plato considered money just a "symbol" devised for the purpose of facilitating exchange (the medium-of-exchange function of money). Hence, domestic currency need not be made of precious metals. Plato indicated, however, that gold and silver might be used internationally to settle trade deficits.[17]

The contributions of Aristotle to monetary theory were also significant. Schumpeter observed that Aristotle recognized the four functions of money—namely, medium of exchange, measure of value, store of value, and standard of deferred payments.[18]

Aristotle also made important contributions to the theory of value. Emil Kauder observes:

> It is generally accepted that Aristotle was the first who created the concept of the value-in-use. [According to Oskar Kraus of Prague] Aristotle had . . . some knowledge of the laws of diminishing utility. Even Menger's theory of imputation . . . can be found in Aristotle.[19]

In summary, Aristotle's holistic approach compelled him to consider that economic activity was teleological. It follows that the "right" (ethical) economic activity was also natural. Hence, "just price," household management (economics) according to the rule of "golden mean," and self-sufficiency of the ideal city-state were all natural. Lending money at interest violated the medium-of-exchange function of money. Therefore, it was unnatural. Unquestionably, Aristotle's teleology contributed greatly to the subsequent development of the doctrine of "natural law."

The World View of Saint Thomas Aquinas

It was a long time from the fifth century B.C. (the Age of Plato) to the thirteenth century A.D. (the time of St. Thomas Aquinas). Many earth-shaking historical events passed during that span of time, such as Alexander's Hellenic civilization, the rise, decline, and fall of the Roman empire, the ensuing "Dark Ages" (approximately between the fifth century and the ninth century A.D.), and the beginning of the "Middle Ages" (approximately between the eleventh and twelfth centuries A.D.). St. Thomas Aquinas (1225–74) was born after the Crusades and the Magna Charta (1215).

During this long period the general approach to philosophy, science, and economics of the "vocal minority" intellegensia (philosophers such as Cicero, Seneca, Pliny, and the Jurists) remained essentially similar to that of Aristotle. The "silent majority" of people (politicians, militarists, merchants, and so forth), however, paid little attention to the voices of the "vocal minority" and continued their pursuits of wealth and a hedonistic life style.

The most important contribution of the Romans was the development of the concept of natural law. According to Peter J. Stanlis, the compilation of Roman law was based completely on natural law, which was regarded by the Roman jurists, such as Gais, Ulpian, and Paulus, as a system of ideal laws founded on intuition and right reason. The Roman tradition of natural law was largely absorbed by St. Ambrose, St. Jerome, St. Augustine, St. Gregory, and other Church Fathers. They reconciled the Roman natural law with Christian "revelation" and "grace," and established the foundations for the development of the Canon Law of the Church. The fusion of classical and Christian thought reached its theological perfection in the *Summa Theologica* of St. Thomas Aquinas.[20]

St. Thomas's Philosophy

St. Thomas's *Summa Theologica* epitomized the scholastic world view of the thirteenth century A.D. Scholasticism was the system of thought that attempted to make philosophy, science, and society completely harmonious with Christian theology. The foundation of Thomism was the baptized Greco-Roman natural law.

Figure I.1. **The world view of St. Thomas**

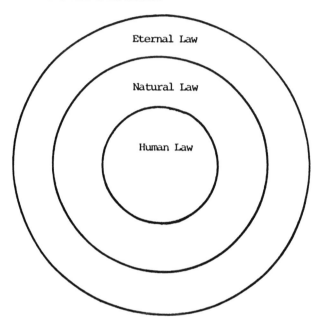

The essence of St. Thomas's world view may be summarized as follows:

(a) There is rational order in nature.

(b) It is the emanation of God's reason and will.

(c) Therefore, it is eternal, unchanging, the embodiment of justice and independent of man's private reason and will.

(d) It is the link between man and God.

Figure I.1 depicts the Thomist world view: The enveloping "Eternal Law" is God's blueprint of the universe. "Natural Law," which regulates all the phenomena of the universe, is derived from "Eternal Law." "Human Law" is a derivative of "Natural Law." Hence, it is also subject to the sanctions of "Eternal Law." On the surface, Thomism appears to neglect the problem of human freedom and the effect of man's actions upon his own fate. But Eric Fromm points out:

Although Aquinas teaches a doctrine of predestination, he never ceases to emphasize freedom of will as one of his fundamental doctrines. To bridge the contrast between the doctrine of freedom and that of predestination, he is obliged to use the most complicated constructions; but, although these constructions do not seem to solve the contradictions satisfactorily, he does not retreat from the doctrine of freedom of the will and of human effort, as being of avail for man's salvation, even though the will itself may need the support of God's grace.[21]

A certain flexibility of Thomism is also manifested in his allowing reason to ascertain some truths of theology without revelation, such as the five logical proofs for the existence of God.[22]

St. Thomas's world view satisfied the ''quest for certainty'' of people in the late Middle Ages. According to the psychological interpretation of Eric Fromm, ''Although a person was not free in the modern sense, neither was he alone and isolated. In having a distinct, unchangeable, and unquestionable place in the social world from the moment of birth, man was rooted in a structuralized whole, and thus life had a meaning which left no place, and no need, for doubt [such as modern man's question: ''Who am I?'']''[23]

This was the general consensus that made it possible for the Thomist Christian Commonwealth to promote justice and peace on earth and mankind's salvation in the world to come. There were unavoidably dissenting voices. The evaporation of the ''consensus'' started in the fourteenth century; in the sixteenth century it completely collapsed.

The Scholastic Approach to Science

St. Thomas's approach to science, similar to that of Aristotle, is focused on the question ''why?'' The approach is holistic and totally rationalistic. Since the laws of nature conform to God's blueprint, the only logical task for science is to understand the reason and will of God. There is no room for experiments. Nature is teleological. Thus, St. Thomas discussed motion from the standpoint of the Aristotelian doctrine of the four causes and thought of it as a manifestation of potentiality seeking its actualization.

St. Thomas also adopted the Ptolemaic system of geocentric astronomy which is compatible with Aristotelian physics. It has been said that the medieval period was concerned mainly with mankind's salvation in the world to come. In such a climate science could not bloom. Sir James Jeans's opinion of medieval science is quite low:

> If science retained any existence through this period, it was a science of a useless kind, which concerned itself with, as we now know, wholly unprofitable quests such as the search for the philosopher's stone and the elixir of life, with alchemy and astrology, with magic and the black arts; its aims were wholly utilitarian and most unworthy.[24]

It should be noted that the scientists of the Renaissance, such as Copernicus, Kepler, Galileo, and Newton, were all believers in God's blueprint for nature. Each sought a better understanding of His design. According to Morris Kline, "It is an irony of history that their researches produced laws which clashed with Church doctrines and that these researches ultimately undermined the Church's domination of thought."[25]

During the lifetime of St. Thomas there were dissenters to the purely rationalistic approach to science. A prominent dissenter was Roger Bacon (1214–94).

St. Thomas's Economics

The holistic approach of St. Thomas concerned economic activity as a teleological process. The basis for the conception is found in the doctrine of the right of dominion, which is explained by Stephan Theodore Worland as follows: Man's final cause is salvation after life. Following the decree of degree of divine providence, "lower creatures exist for the sake of the higher," the ultimate purpose of the latter coincides with that of man.

Thus, man exercises his domain over nature.[26]

At the center of the normative economics of St. Thomas is the doctrine of "just price." Society is considered as an organism. Purchases and sales are social transactions and social transactions are governed by justice (commutative justice).

What are the determinants of the "just price"? On the supply side, St. Thomas believed that the reward of the producers should be proportional to their effort. In the words of Walter A. Weiskopf, "This principle is the historical and psychological root of the labor theory of value."[27]

This basic principle of economic ethics of St. Thomas prompted Richard H. Tawney (1880–1962) to make the following colorful statement: "The true descendant of the doctrines of Aquinas is the labor theory of value. The last of the Schoolmen was Karl Marx."[28]

It should be noted, however, that St. Thomas did not totally neglect the demand side of "just price" doctrine. Following Aristotle, he also considered "value in use" as the other "Marshallian blade" in price determination. Worland explains this point clearly as follows: St. Thomas considered that it is human need that gives rise to the exchange value of commodities. He cited an illustration borrowed from St. Augustine: "If prices of things are not established according to human need, a mouse would be more valuable than a pearl."[29]

The Disintegration of the Medieval World View

The scholastic synthesis of St. Thomas began to erode in the fourteenth century. The first sign of erosion was the philosophical dissension of the Franciscan Schoolmen (Aquinas belonged to the Dominican Order). The leader of the Franciscans was Duns Scotus (1270–1308), who disputed the Thomist rationalization of some of the religious beliefs such as the five logical proofs of the existence of God. Scotus argued that faith is an act of individual will, not an act of intellect. Religion should be accepted on faith or rejected entirely. This argument has often been referred to as "voluntarism."

The most important Franciscan schoolman was William Occam (or Ockham), who was born probably between the years 1280 and 1290 and died in 1349, probably of the black death. He was an exponent of Nominalism, which emphasized individuals, empiricism, and the secularization of philosophy, whereas the moderate realist, St. Thomas stressed ordered hierarchy, group control, and a harmony between faith and reason. From the standpoint of economic analysis, one of Occam's maxims is most relevant to the development of utility theory. The maxim states that "one can profitably get rid of all alleged entities the existence of which cannot be verified in experience."[30] This maxim subsequently acquired the name of "Occam's razor," or principle of economy. "Occam's razor" had been used at first by ordinal-utility theorists to "shave off" the philosophical underpinnings of the theory, namely, Utilitarianism. Subsequently they invoked the same principle to purge cardinalism from utility theory. The ghost of Occam may even have guided the hands of Samuelson in his formulation of the celebrated theory of "revealed preference."

During the following three centuries many profound political, economic, and intellectual changes took place that hastened the collapse of the medieval cosmology and with it, the "certainty" of the Thomist "natural law" doctrine was also destroyed. The quest for the "new certainty" was launched by the philosophers and scientists of the Renaissance. This lofty objective was finally attained by the grand synthesis of Sir Isaac Newton in 1687. A mechanical interpretation of the universe based on Newtonian mechanics finally replaced the ancient and medieval organic view of nature. During the Age of Enlightenment, philosophy, physics, and society were once again unified.

The Newtonian "mechanical world view" and its influence on the development of economic analyses are the subjects of chapter 1 of this book. There are many good books on the relationship between philosophy and physics.[31] There are also excellent books explaining the influence of philosophy on economics.[32] But to the best of our knowledge (which may be limited indeed), so far there has been no text relating the implications of Newtonian mechanics to contemporary economic models.[33] The outstanding feature of this chapter is that it pinpoints the influence of Newtonian mechanics on contemporary economic models, both static and dynamic, that are generally omitted from books of the above-mentioned categories. In addition, the philosophical underpinning of the representative economic models is also considered.

Chapter 2 considers the first important assault on the Newtonian world machine by the so-called "Romantic Revolt" against the shackles of the "Age of Reason." The original inspiration for the romantic alternative approach to philosophy was the German transcendental idealism of Immanuel Kant (1724–1804). Kant's seminal book *Critique of Pure Reason* (1781) exposed the limitations of science and rationalism. The Kantian emphasis is on the subjective and ideal rather than the objective and real. In fact, he opened the flood gate for the subsequent romantics to believe almost anything they wanted to believe. The Kantian philosophy fortified their belief that nature is not a machine but a living spirit, a vast will, and a wiser teacher than any scientific treatise. The English romantic poets prescribed the communion with nature as the first step for the quest for the recovery of the "whole man." The philosophy of Georg Wilhelm Friedrich Hegel (1770–1831) asserted that history is a process of "becoming"—the march of the spirit toward freedom. The Hegelian idealism reflects the romantics' inclination to champion biology because the notion of organism provides them with the metaphor for much of their speculative thought. It appears that the romantics were reaching back to some aspects of the Aristotelian and Thomist view of nature as organic. There is, however, at least one major difference between the two organic views. The romantics glorified passion, whereas Aristotle and St. Thomas, like the philosophers of the Enlightenment, worshiped reason.

Although the romantics were inclined to reject Newtonian mechanics and to champion biology instead, they did not formulate any systematic scientific theory of organic evolution. Their theories of evolution were essentially philosophical. Jean Baptiste Lamarck (1744–1829) was the first to introduce a coherent hypothesis of organic evolution in 1809. In 1859 Charles Darwin published the *Origin of Species*. These important advances in the biological sciences came after the heyday of the Romantic movement (the first half of the nineteenth century).

In spite of the spirited onslaught of the romantics, the Newtonian mechanistic world view remained entrenched. Nevertheless, the Romantic movement left an important imprint on the development of philosophy and the evolution of economics. Chapter 2 of this book deals with the interrelationships between economics, philosophy, and physics. Once again, Newtonian physics lurks behind the biological sciences. As pointed out by Paul Davies, "One hears it said that biology is just a branch of chemistry, which is in turn just a branch of physics."[34] Chapter 2 also includes a brief review of the impact of the Romantic movement on Karl Marx's 1844 *Manuscripts*, the "Utopian Socialism," August Comte's positivism, the German Historical School of Economics, and John Stuart Mill.

The second wave of attack on Newtonian mechanics and the mechanistic world view was the advance of thermodynamics in physics. As mentioned earlier, Newtonian time is symmetrical: the arrow of time can point in either direction; there is no distinction between "time forwards" and "time backwards." Darwinian theory of evolution involves a distinctly unidirectional "arrow of time." However, as observed by Nicholas Georgescu-Roegen, "of all the time's arrows suggested thus far for the biological world . . . the suggested attributes are not ordinarily measurable. . . . It is physics again that supplies the only clear example of an evolutionary law: the Second Law of Thermodynamics, called also the Entropy Law."[35] The purpose of chapter 3 of this book is to consider the impact of the entropy law on the Newtonian mechanistic world view and on orthodox economics modeled after Newtonian physics.

The two laws of thermodynamics gave the mechanistic world view a severe blow, but did not topple Newtonian mechanics.

Furthermore, the early prognosis of the entropy arrow of time was too gloomy. The German physicist Hermann von Helmholtz in 1854 predicted the "heat death" of the universe. Ludwig Boltzmann was the first to deliver the universe from its impending doom by introducing probability into the entropy law. According to Ilya Prigogine and Isabelle Stengers, "Boltzmann's results signify that irreversible thermodynamic change is a change toward states of increasing probability and that the attractor state is a macroscopic state corresponding to maximum probability. This takes us far beyond Newton. For the first time a physical concept has been explained in terms of probability."[36]

The Newtonian mechanics, however, continued to be the basis of the mainstream world view. Thus, Georgescu-Roegen writes:

> A curious event in the history of economic thought is that, years after the mechanistic dogma has lost its supremacy in physics and its grip on the philosophical world, the founders of the neoclassical school set out to erect an economic science after the pattern of mechanics— in the words of Jevons, as "the mechanics of utility and self-interest."[37]

It was not until the 1960s that the two laws of thermodynamics became the scientific foundation of modern antigrowth theories. The works of Georgescu-Roegen, Herman E. Daly, E.F. Schumacher, Kenneth E. Boulding, and other antigrowth theorists are considered in chapter 3.

The basic convictions of Newtonian physics have been mostly replaced by the Second Revolution in physics. The Second Revolution consists of two earth-shaking theories: the theory of relativity and quantum theory. Albert Einstein's relativity theory is the subject of chapter 4; quantum theory is considered in chapter 5.

Chapter 4 begins with the generating motive of the whole theory of relativity. As pointed out by Bertrand Russell:

> physics must be concerned with those features which a physical process has in common for all observers, since such features alone can be regarded as belonging to the physical occurrence itself. This

> requires that the laws of phenomenon should be the same whether
> the phenomena are described as they appear to one observer or an-
> other. This simple principle is the generating motive of the whole
> theory of relativity.[38]

It is this "generating motive" that lies behind the first fundamental principle of Einstein's Special Theory of Relativity
(1905) which states: "All inertial frames are equivalent with respect to all laws of physics."[39]

The second fundamental principle of Einstein's Special Theory is perhaps the trickiest aspect of the entire theory; it states:
"The speed of light in empty space always has the same value,
$c = 3000,000$ km/sec." The rationale of this principle may be
stated as follows: Newtonian physics asserted that there was no
ambiguity in saying that two events at distant places happened
at the same time (or absolute simultaneity). This assertion was
based on the assumption of absolute space and absolute time.
Furthermore, Newtonian physics implied that there was no limiting velocity for the propagation of all signs. Hence, the laws of
Newton can be applied in the same way, whatever the scale of the
objects. This is the reason for Newtonian physics' claim to universality. That is to say that the motions of atoms, planets, and
stars are governed by the same laws. Another subtle implication
of Newtonian physics is that the observer only observes from the
outside of the physical universe.

Einstein's second fundamental principle was introduced to attain three objectives: (1) The new universal constant, c, limits the
region in space that affects an observer's propagation of signals.
Put differently, the constant velocity of light in empty space im-
poses the limiting velocity for the propagation of signals that
cannot be transgressed by any observer. Thus, one can no longer
define the absolute simultaneity of two distant events. In other
words, one can only talk about relative simultaneity, which can
be defined only in terms of a given reference frame. An analog of
this limit is the budget constraint of an individual consumer in
microeconomics. It defines the individual consumption frontier.

Any point beyond the frontier is the unreachable star. (2) The
Newtonian physics' claim to universality is demolished by
the new universal constant. And (3) the new universal constant
highlights the fact that the observer is situated within the observed world. Therefore man's dialog with nature is carried on
within nature.

With the fall of the concept of absolute simultaneity, the other
Newtonian concepts, such as absolute time, absolute space, and
absolute matter also collapse. Einstein introduced the revolutionary concept of the four-dimensional space-time continuum to
replace the Newtonian separation of space and time. His most
famous formula for the equivalence of mass and energy, $E = mc^2$,
does away with the Newtonian concept of absolute matter.

Einstein realized that his Special Theory of Relativity was
inconsistent with the Newtonian theory of gravity. His special
theory is restricted to inertial phenomena (light is an electromagnetic phenomenon). Following his faith in the invariance principle as stated in the preceding paragraphs, Einstein attempted to
consider accelerating frames of reference and to incorporate
gravitational phenomena. The result was the General Theory of
Relativity (1915).

The invariance principle discovered by Einstein in the General
Theory is "the Principle of Equivalence of Gravitation and Inertia," which states that there is no difference between the motion
produced by inertial forces such as acceleration, recoil, centrifugal forces, etc., from gravitation. He made the revolutionary suggestion that one should stop thinking about the idea of force of
gravity altogether and use instead the language of non-Euclidean
geometry in the discussion of gravitational effects. In other
words, gravitation is geometry. The so-called "force of gravity"
is simply a consequence of the fact that the space-time continuum is curved (or warped) by the distribution of mass and energy
in it. The renowned American physicist John Wheeler gives
Einstein's notion the following colorful description: "Space tells
matter how to move and matter tells space how to curve."[40]

Chapter 4 closes with (a) a brief survey of the views of Sir

James Jeans, Bertrand Russell, Hans Reichanbach, and David Bohm on the philosophical consequences of the theory of relativity, and (b) some observations on the impact of relativity theory in the area of economics.

The subject of chapter 5 is quantum mechanics and its impact on economics and philosophy. It has been generally recognized among physicists that quantum mechanics implies a much more radical break with the past than did the conclusions of relativity theory. For Einstein's revolutionary theory still retains the same ambition of classical physics to achieve a complete description of nature. This lofty objective is like searching for the "philosopher's stone." Among other things, it would require that the laws of the macroworld be consistent with those of the microworld. The puzzle of subatomic anarchy depicted by quantum mechanics crushed Einstein's valiant quest for the "Holy Grail."

Quantum mechanics reveals that electrons behave like waves —not a wave of any sort of substance, but a wave of probability (like a "crime wave" for example). Thus, quantum mechanics is basically a statistical theory. Furthermore, the probability is inherent in a quantum particle which does not have any well-defined values. This inherent vagueness or fuzziness leads directly to Werner Heisenberg's famous principle of uncertainty, or indeterminacy, which states that the position and momentum of a subatomic particle cannot be simultaneously determined.

The implication of the uncertain relations led Niels Bohr to formulate his "principle of complementarity" which may be considered as the centerpiece of the "Copenhagen Interpretation of Quantum Mechanics." According to this principle, the wave and particle behavior of subatomic particles are really complementary aspects of the same subatomic particles. Furthermore, the very act of our observation changes the position or the momentum of the subatomic particle under observation. Thus, the observer, the apparatus of observation, and the subatomic particle must be considered an indivisible whole of the experiment. The inherent wholeness of the process is one of the main features of quantum mechanics. The approach is unmistakably holistic or synthetic, as opposed to analytic or reductionist, because it treats systems as a whole. Another frustrating aspect of the process is that we can only know the result of the experiment. There is no way for us to know what a subatomic particle is doing when we are not looking at it. In other words, it implies that there is no Newtonian clockwork that ticks away regardless of whether we look at it or not.

A new "Holy Grail" soon appeared to be sought after by the quantum "crusaders." This new "Grail" was the synthesis of relativity theory and quantum mechanics. Most promising among the various searchers for the new synthesis is Richard P. Feynman's formulation of "quantum electrodynamics" (QED), which subsumes the four fundamental forces, namely gravity, electromagnetism, the weak nuclear forces, and the strong nuclear forces, under the interaction of particles in the "quantum field."

Chapter 5 closes with some observations on the impact of quantum mechanics on economics and philosophy.

Chapter 6 considers the emerging new science, Chaos. The recent advance of fractal geometry and chaos theory contributes greatly to bridging the gap between chance and necessity. It also reinforces the probabilistic interpretation of the reality of quantum mechanics. In the words of Paul Davies, "the universe is in some sense open; it cannot be known what new levels of variety or complexity may be in store."[41]

This chapter begins with a short history of the development of chaos theory, followed by a brief explanation of the mathematics of Mandelbrot fractals and other related concepts. The impact of chaos theory is the beginning of an integration process of different scientific disciplines. Second, chaos reaffirms the message of quantum mechanics about the limitation of human knowledge of the universe around us. Lastly, chaos theory calls for a new scientific methodology of making predictions and testing the predictions against experimental data.

The recent works on chaos have prompted the reconsideration

of the following time-honored philosophical questions: (a) being and becoming; (b) chance and necessity (or free will and determinism); (c) order and disorder; (d) mind and matter; (e) time and reality; and (f) the clashes of doctrines between physics and biology.

Relativity, quantum, and chaos theories have laid the scientific foundation for a new synthesis that would provide more positive and optimistic answers to the above-mentioned philosophical questions. The emerging new synthesis starts with a new view of evolution. As observed by Karl Popper and John Eccles, "the new view of evolution suggests that the universe has never ceased to be creative, or inventive."[42] In Eric Jantsch's words, "the new paradigm of evolution is a complex, but holistic dynamic phenomenon of an universal unfolding of order which becomes manifested in many ways, as matter and energy, information and complexity, consciousness and self-reflexion. It is no longer necessary to assume a special life force (such as Bergson's élan vital or prana of Hinduism) separate from the physical forces."[43] In other words, in the emerging new synthesis, "being" and "becoming," "mind" and "matter," "order" and "disorder," "irreversible time" and "reversible time" are not irreconcilable opposites. Rather, they are complementary. "Natural history may also be understood as the evolution of consciousness or evolution of the mind."[44]

Similar views are also expressed by Ilya Prigogine and Isabelle Stengers.[45] On the question of "time and reality," Prigogine and Stengers emphasize that irreversible time makes its appearance only in the regions of chaos of dynamic systems. For under such regimes of randomness, the difference between past and future would be highlighted and therefore "irreversible time" replaces "reversible time" under equilibrium conditions. Since "closed systems" may coexist with an "open" universe, "reversibility" and "irreversibility" of time could be complementary.

On the question of "chance and necessity," the two authors' idea of dissipative structure avoided the traditional either/or controversies. Their revision of the entropy law, together with their incorporation of the "living vacuum" theory of Heisenberg's principle of uncertainty, enabled Prigogine and Stengers to assert that matter is no longer the passive substance described in classical physical physics. The new concept of "active matter" supports their views of a "new dialogue of man with nature."

The self-organizing dynamics of Prigogine-Stengers-Jantsch also overcomes the "mind/matter duality" as well as the conflicts of doctrines between biology and physics. The emerging new synthesis may be viewed as another illustration of the main thesis of this book.

Chapter 6 closes with some observations on the subject of chaos and economics. We begin with William J. Baumol and Jess Benhabib's research on the roots of economists' interest in chaos today.[46] Next, we consider the applications of chaos theory to economics by Jean-Michel Grandmont, William A. Brock, and B.B. Mandelbrot. The chapter closes with the views of Guy Routh on economics and chaos.[47]

The concluding chapter 7 contains the authors' view on the prospective future of economics in the light of relativity, quantum, and chaos theories. We don't pretend to know the answer to this difficult problem. In order to find some clues that will shed some light on the situation, we proceed first to set the question in the context of some leading suggested reconstructions of economics since the conquest of the mechanistic world view. The suggested reconstructions are grouped under two categories. The first category covers some suggested methodological revisions without revolutionary "paradigm shifts." Some of the important arguments for revolutionary "paradigm shifts" are grouped under the second category.

The research programs of modern economics surveyed under the first category constitute the ongoing activity involving the refining and sharpening of tools for problem solving. They are reductionist and analytical. The Newtonian mechanistic world view is taken for granted.

All of the suggested reconstructions of economics under the

second category are against mechanism. Practically all of them are in favor of a holistic and synthetic approach to economic problems.

Which path should economists take in the future? It is not a clear-cut, either/or question. In pondering this problem we found a pearl of wisdom in the words of Paul Davies: "reductionism and holism are really two complementary rather than conflicting paradigms. There has always been a place for both in properly conducted science."[48] We would, therefore, suggest that in the short run, the economics profession will continue the ongoing research activity of problem solving with the reductionist approach.

In the long run, the problem is more involved. The economics profession must take into consideration (a) the changing perception of reality as a result of the new physics, and (b) the emerging "new paradigm" hinted by Prigogine-Stengers-Jantsch (see chapter 5). We should not overlook the fact that "closed systems" may coexist with an "open universe" and that "mind and matter," "order and disorder," "irreversibility and reversibility of time" are complementary. It appears that the emerging new paradigm may be considered as a generalized "principle of complementarity" of Niels Bohr. There is no doubt that in the long run economics as well as other social sciences have to adopt a holistic approach. It is easy to say that holism is the right approach in the long run. But adopting it is very difficult in practice. Perhaps a workable solution to this long-run problem is to revitalize the interdisciplinary approach in the spirit of the physicist Geoffry Chew's "bootstrap approach." No simple canonical model for all disciplines is advocated here. What is required is that each discipline should develop its own models, which should, however, be mutually consistent with those constructed by other related disciplines. The way to attain this objective is through constant dialogue among the participants so that insights will be shared by all. Such an undertaking will be successful when it is accompanied by the participants' humility and generosity.

Notes

1. Sir James Jeans, *Physics and Philosophy* (Ann Arbor: University of Michigan Press, 1966), p. 2.

2. Paul Davies, *Superforce: The Search for a Grand Unified Theory of Nature* (New York: Simon & Schuster, 1985), p. 3.

3. Paul Davidson, *Money and the Real World* (New York: John Wiley & Sons, 1972; 2nd ed. 1978). Also see Ching-Yao Hsieh and Stephen L. Mangum, *A Search for Synthesis in Economic Theory* (Armonk, NY: M.E. Sharpe, 1986), pp. 170–77.

4. John Dewey, *The Quest for Certainty* (New York: G.P. Putnam's Sons, 1929, Capricorn Books ed. 1960), p. 16.

5. Philip J. Davis and Reuben Hersh, *The Mathematical Experience* (Boston: Houghton Mifflin, 1981), p. 325.

6. Ibid.

7. Morris Kline, *Mathematics in Western Culture* (New York: Oxford University Press, 1964), pp. 55–56.

8. Oswald Spengler, *The Decline of the West*, vol. 1, trans. by Charles Francis Atkinson (New York: Alfred A. Knopf, 1926), p. 183.

9. David Bohm, *Unfolding Meaning* (London: Ark Paperbacks, 1987), p. 1.

10. Stephen W. Hawking, *A Brief History of Time* (New York: Bantam Books, 1988), p. 15.

11. Ibid., p. 18.

12. Paul Davies, *The Cosmic Blueprint* (New York: Simon & Schuster, 1988), p. 7.

13. See chapter 7 of this book.

14. See George Dalton, ed., *Primitive, Archaic and Modern Economies: Essays of Karl Polanyi* (Garden City, NY: Doubleday, 1968), p. 65.

15. Ibid., pp. 70–71.

16. Ibid., p. 106.

17. Joseph A. Schumpeter, *History of Economic Analysis* (New York: Oxford University Press, 1954), p. 56.

18. Ibid., pp. 62–63.

19. Emil Kauder, *A History of Marginal Utility Theory* (Princeton, NJ: Princeton University Press, 1965), pp. 15–16.

20. Peter J. Stanlis, *Edmund Burke and the Natural Law* (Ann Arbor: University of Michigan Press, 1965), p. 9.

21. Eric Fromm, *Escape from Freedom* (New York: Discus Books, Avon, 1941), p. 88.

22. See Bertrand Russell, *A History of Western Philosophy* (New York: Simon & Schuster, 1945), p. 445.

23. Fromm, *Escape from Freedom*, p. 58.

24. Sir James Jeans, *Physics and Philosophy*, p. 19.

25. Morris Kline, *Mathematics in Western Culture*, p. 97.

26. See Stephen Theodore Worland, *Scholasticism and Welfare Economics* (Notre Dame: University of Notre Dame Press, 1967), pp. 47–48.

27. Walter A. Weisskopf, *The Psychology of Economics* (Chicago: University of Chicago Press, 1955), p. 26.

28. Richard H. Tawney, *Religion and the Rise of Capitalism* (New York: New American Library, 1947), pp. 38–39.

29. Worland, *Scholasticism and Welfare Economics*, pp. 218–19.

30. These are the words of Frederick C. Colpeston, *Medieval Philosophy* (New York: Harper & Row, 1961), p. 125.

31. See Sir James Jeans, *Philosophy and Physics*; Werner Heisenberg, *Physics and Philosophy* (New York: Harper & Row, 1958); Max Planck, *The Philosophy of Physics* (New York: W.W. Norton, 1936); *Philosophic Problems of Nuclear Science* (Greenwich, CT: Fawcett Publications, 1952); David Bohm, *Wholeness and the Implicate Order* (London: Ark Paperbacks, 1983); and Fritjof Capra, *The Tao of Physics* (New York: Bantam Books, 1977).

32. See Piero V. Mini, *Philosophy and Economics* (Gainesville: University Press of Florida, 1974); Homa Katouzian, *Ideology and Method in Economics* (New York: New York University Press, 1980); Mark Blaug, *The Methodology of Economics* (Cambridge: Cambridge University Press, 1980); Lawrence A. Boland, *The Foundations of Economic Method* (London: Allen and Unwin, 1982); and Sir John Hicks, *Causality in Economics* (New York: Basic Books, 1979).

33. There are two books relating physics to economics: (1) Philip Mirowski, *Against Mechanism* (Totowa, NJ: Roman & Littlefield, 1988), esp. Part I; and (2) Fritjof Capra, *The Turning Point* (New York: Bantam Books, 1983), esp. chap. 7. It should be noted that the presentations of these two books are quite different from that of our book.

34. Davies, *The Cosmic Blueprint*, p. 98.

35. Nicholas Georgescu-Roegen, *The Entropy Law and the Economic Process* (Cambridge, MA: Harvard University Press, 1971), pp. 128–29.

36. Ilya Prigogine and Isabelle Stengers, *Order out of Chaos* (New York: Bantam Books, 1984), p. 124.

37. Nicholas Georgescu-Roegen, "The Entropy Law and the Economic Problem." In Herman E. Daly, ed., *Economics, Biology, Ethics: Essays Toward a Steady-State Economy* (San Francisco: W.H. Freeman, 1980), p. 37.

38. Bertrand Russell, *The ABC of Relativity* (London: Allen & Unwin, 1958), pp. 22–23.

39. These are the words of A.P. French, *Special Relativity* (New York: W.W. Norton, 1968), p. 72.

40. Quoted by Paul Davies, *Other Worlds* (New York: Simon & Schuster, 1980), p. 50.

41. Davies, *The Cosmic Blueprint*, p. 56.

42. Karl Popper and John Eccles, *The Self and Its Brain* (Berlin: Springer International, 1977), p. 61.

43. Eric Jantsch, *The Self-Organizing Universe* (Oxford: Pergamon Press, 1980), p. 307.

44. Ibid., p. 307.

45. Prigogine and Stengers, *Order out of Chaos*.

46. William J. Baumol and Jess Benhabib, "Chaos: Significance, Mechanism, and Economic Applications," *Journal of Economic Perspectives 3*, 1 (Winter 1989): pp. 77–105.

47. Jean-Michel Grandmont, "On Endogenous Competitive Business Cycles," *Econometrica 53* (1985); William A. Brock, "Distinguishing Random and Deterministic Systems: Abridged Version," *Journal of Economic Theory 40* (1986); B.B. Mandelbrot, *The Fractal Geometry of Nature* (San Francisco: W.H. Freeman, 1982); and "The Variation of Certain Speculative Prices," *Journal of Business* (1963), pp. 394–419; Guy Routh, "Economics and Chaos," *Challenge* (July–August 1989).

48. Davies, *The Cosmic Blueprint*, pp. 198–99.

Economics, Philosophy, and Physics

Chapter 1

Newtonian Physics, Philosophy, and Economics

The medieval world view was severely damaged by two revolutions: the Copernican Revolution in astronomy (1543) and the Cartesian Revolution in philosophy (1637). "The Copernican Revolution," as pointed out by Thomas S. Kuhn, "was a revolution in ideas, a transformation in man's conception of the universe and of his own relation to it. Again and again this history of Renaissance thought has been proclaimed an epochal turning point in the intellectual development of Western man."[1] In other words, the Copernican Revolution paved the way for the conception of the mechanical world view.

There had been two strands of thought in the quest for new certainty before Newton. In his *Novum Organum* (1620), Francis Bacon (1561–1626) launched a skillful attack on scholasticism and urged philosophers to adopt the empirical method. The other strand was Réné Descartes's (1596–1650) rationalist quest for certain knowledge. In *Discourse upon Method* (1637), Descartes started with radical doubt of everything and ended with a firm belief in the view that nature was a perfect machine governed by exact mathematical laws (Descartes's "universal mathematics"). Thus, a new order of the universe was established and a new language had to be developed for the description of this new order.

Descartes invented analytical geometry (the Cartesian coordinates) for this purpose. David Bohm observes:

> To use coordinates is in effect to order our perception and our thinking. . . . [O]nce men were ready to conceive of the universe as a machine, they would naturally tend to take the order of coordinates as a universally relevant one, valid for all basic descriptions in physics.[2]

This idea is depicted by Figure 1.1: in order to specify the position of a particle it is necessary to know three distances (space has three dimensions), namely (a) length, represented by the Cartesian axis X in Figure 1.1, (b) breadth, represented by Cartesian axis Y, and (c) height, represented by the Cartesian axis Z. The three distances, X, Y, and Z, are called Cartesian coordinates. The position of the particle G is expressed in the form of (X, Y, Z). The use of the Cartesian coordinates was implicit in Newtonian physics. The introduction of the Cartesian coordinates was indeed an important contribution of the Cartesian Revolution.

Another salient feature of the Cartesian Revolution, which is relevant to the subsequent development of economic analysis, was the so-called "reductionist methodology." According to Descartes, certain knowledge should be achieved through intuition and deduction. This methodology is succinctly summarized by Fritjof Capra:

> Descartes' method is analytic. It consists of breaking up thoughts and problems into pieces and in arranging these in their logical order. This analytic method of reasoning is probably Descartes' greatest contribution to science. It has become an essential characteristic of modern scientific thought and has proved extremely useful in the development of scientific theories and the realization of complex technological projects.[3]

A third feature of Cartesian philosophy was the so-called "mind-matter duality." According to Descartes, there are two independent and separate realms of nature. One of the realms is

Figure 1.1. **The use of Cartesian coordinates to fix the position of a particle in space**

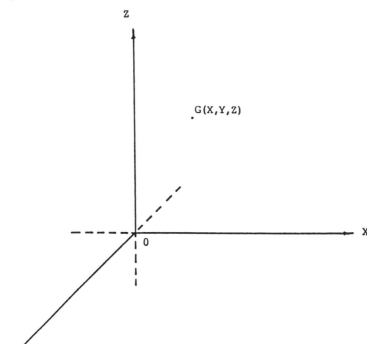

the realm of mind; he referred to this as "*res cognitas.*" The other realm is the realm of matter, which he called "*res extensa.*" This Cartesian duality led to two tenets of Western sciences: (a) the observer of the physical universe only observes but never disturbs; and (b) the physical universe is a machine governed by exact mathematical laws.

In the realm of natural sciences, the Copernican heliocentric astronomy was subsequently refined by Johann Kepler (1571–1630). Among other things, Kepler emphasized that the path of each planet is not circular as depicted by Copernicus, but rather is an ellipse with the sun slightly off center at a point known as the focus of the ellipse.

The most famous contemporary of Kepler was Galileo Galilei (1564–1642). It is interesting to note that William Shakespeare was born in the same year as Galileo and that Isaac Newton was born in the year he died. It was Galileo who finally broke the lingering bondage of Aristotelian physics and medieval scholasticism. Thus, Galileo, more than any other single person, was responsible for the birth of modern science.

Galileo's devotion to obtain quantitative description of nature may be best illustrated by his law of falling bodies: $d = 1/2gt^2$, where d denotes the number of feet the body falls; g stands for the constant acceleration of a body dropped in a vacuum ($g = 32$ feet per second); and t is time in seconds. Thus, the law may be rewritten as $d = 16t^2$.

Galileo did not offer explainations for why phenomena occur, such as Heron's famous explanation that "nature abhors a vacuum." His formula is precise and quantitatively complete in a way that is characteristic of modern science.

It may be said that it was Galileo who planted the seed of what John Hicks called the "New Causality":

> Causality can only be asserted, in terms of New Causality, if we have some theory, or generalization, into which observed events can be fitted; to suppose that we have theories into which all events can be fitted, is to make a large claim indeed.[4]

François Quesnay's tableau économique (1758), the quantity theory of money elucidated by John Locke (1632–1704), David Hume (1711–76), and Richard Cantillon (1680–1734), as well as David Ricardo's one-sector "corn model" (1815) brought forth during the so-called "corn laws controversy" were all in line with the "New Causality." Even today economists are still attempting to fit observed events into some mathematical models.

Newton's Grand Synthesis

The climax of the intellectual revolution in philosophy as well as in science was a movement that has come to be known as the

Enlightenment, which has had profound effects in shaping the modern mind. Isaac Newton (1642–1727) was one of the real founders of the movement; another one was John Locke (1632–1704). It was Newton who introduced the proper mixture of Bacon's empiricism and Cartesian rationalism and developed the methodology which physical and social sciences have adopted ever since.

The connection between mechanics and mathematics had been perceived by Archimedes and developed by Galileo. Newton went beyond Galileo and developed a comprehensive system of mechanics dealing with motion of all types, both on earth and in heaven.

The Newtonian mechanics may be stated as follows: Newton visualized the universe as a collection of particles (or basic matter) in motion. According to K.R. Atkins, Newton's first law of motion, as presented in his *Principia*, states:

> In the absence of any interaction with the rest of the universe, a body would either remain at rest or move continually in the same straight line with a constant velocity.[5]

This state of rest or motion would be changed by the interactions of the particles. Forces generated by the interactions would produce accelerations and distortions of the particles' paths. Newton's second law of motion gives a precise definition of the concept of force:

> If a body of mass, m, has an acceleration, a, then the force acting on it is defined as the product of its mass and its accelerations. Force = Mass × Acceleration: $F = ma$.[6]

Newton's third law of motion states:

> If body 1 exerts on body 2 a force F_{12}, then body 2 exerts on body 1 a force F_{21}, which is equal in magnitude but exactly opposite in direction. $F_{12} = F_{21}$.[7]

Using the concept of force, Newton was able to express the law governing gravitational interactions in a particularly elegant and symmetrical form, $F = GM_1M_2/R^2$, which states that every particle of matter in the universe attracts every other particle with a force, F, that varies in direct proportion to the product of their masses, M_1M_2, and inversely as the square of the distance between them, R^2. The letter G in the formula stands for "gravitational constant," which is one of the constants in nature.

Newton's universal law of gravitation established the existence of universal laws of mathematics. It also implies the uniformity and invariability of nature. As Paul Davies points out:

> It came to be realized that a startling conclusion must follow. If every particle of matter is subject to Newton's laws, so that its motion is entirely determined by the initial conditions and the pattern of forces arising from all the other particles, then everything that happens in the universe, right down to the smallest movement of an atom, must be fixed in complete detail.[8]

This arresting inference was made explicit by Pierre Simon, Marquis de Laplace (1749–1827), in his claim that everything that has ever happened in the universe, everything that is happening now, and everything that ever will happen, has been unalterably determined since the first instant of time.

Laplace's claim has frequently been referred to as "Laplacian deterministic predictability." The aspiration of Laplace is still apparent in contemporary growth theory. The opening paragraph of Edwin Burmeister and A. Rodney Dobell's excellent text, *Mathematical Theories of Economic Growth*, provides ample evidence of this point:

> The mathematician Laplace is reputed to have said, "Give me only the equations of motion, and I will show you the future of the Universe." Likewise, economists studying the evolution of a large general equilibrium system ask only for the equation of motion in order to bring their work to completion.[9]

Figure 1.2. **A simplified schematic representation of Newtonian cosmology**

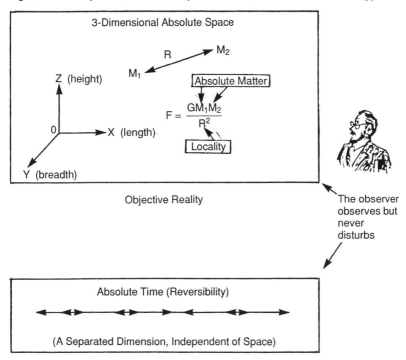

Newtonian mechanics is a description of the dynamic aspect of the universe. Change was treated by Newton as smooth and continuous. He needed a new mathematical tool to describe such motion. "Contrary to the popular belief that genius breaks radically with its age," pointed out by Morris Kline, "three of the greatest seventeenth-century minds, Pierre Fermar, Isaac Newton, and Gottfried Wilhelm Leibniz, each working independently of the other, became absorbed in the problems of calculus."[10] Although Newton did not complete the development of differential calculus, the Newtonian paradigm was deeply rooted in that branch of mathematics.

Newton's laws implied absolute space, absolute time, and absolute matter. Space remains invariable; it only provides the stage for the drama of moving particles under the direction of Newton's laws of motion and the universal law of gravitation. Hence, it is called absolute space. Absolute time means that time is completely separated from and independent of space, and that its function is to measure the interval of time between events. This interval of time would be invariable whoever measured it with a good clock. As aptly put by Paul Davies,

> Newtonian time derives from a very basic property of the laws of motion: they are reversible. That is, the laws do not distinguish "time forwards" from "time backwards"; the arrow of time can point either way. From the standpoint of these laws, a movie played in reverse would be a perfectly acceptable sequence of real events.[11]

Absolute matter implies that the mass of a particle is fixed. It would remain the same whether at rest or in motion. A larger mass only requires a greater force to move it.

Figure 1.2 is a simplified schematic representation of Newtonian cosmology.

The explicit and implicit assumptions of the Newtonian conception of reality are:

1. Absolute space, absolute time, absolute matter (M_1 and M_2 in Figure 1.2);
2. Force of gravitation;
3. Smooth and continuous motion;
4. Reductionist methodology which depends upon *linearity* (a linear system is one in which the whole is simply the sum of its parts), *deterministic predictability* (which also depends upon linearity), and *objective reality* (the observer observes but never disturbs).

Newton's Influence on the Enlightenment

The word, enlightenment, means knowledge. As Nicholas Capaldi points out, "It meant specifically self-knowledge or an understanding of human nature, and it conveys a sense of usefulness of that knowledge. How the Enlightenment came to signify the knowledge of man's nature and how that knowledge might be used to improve the human condition are also the story of the growth of the social sciences.''[12] Economics in the modern sense and other social sciences were born in the Enlightenment.

There are so many great seminal minds in the Age of Enlightenment, that it is beyond the scope of this book to consider them all. For our purpose, it will be sufficient to discuss only John Locke for the following reasons:

1. Locke's philosophy is in perfect harmony with Newtonian mechanics. According to Crane Brinton, ''Locke seemed to show men the way Newton's great successes could be applied to the study of human affairs. Together, Newton and Locke set up those great clusters of ideas, Nature and Reason, which were to the Enlightenment what such clusters of ideas as grace, salvation, and predestination were to traditional Christianity.''[13]

2. Locke's science of human nature had revolutionary implications for politics, economics, and education. In his *Essay Concerning Human Understanding* (1690), Locke argued that there are no innate ideas (as stated by Descartes) in men. Man is born with a mind that resembles a ''tabula rasa''—a blank table. According to Locke, man should be modeled after the mechanical view of nature. All mental activity is initiated by external stimuli. These stimuli produce sensations in the mind of the subject, until sensation begets memory and memory begets ideas. This is the psychology of associationism. The revolutionary implication of the Lockean epistemology and psychology on education is succinctly stated by Capaldi: ''Men could be completely refashioned and reformed through appropriate conditioning and education.''[14] The education of John Stuart Mill under his father James Mill is a prime example of the Enlightenment faith in the perfectibility of man.

3. The Lockean science of human nature removed God from human affairs (no more innate ideas and ''original sins''). Thus, pure self-interest, which is analogous to Newtonian force of gravity, becomes the sole basis for economic activity as well as

for the establishment of the state. Self-interest as the motivating force of economic activity had been well documented in classical and neoclassical economics and in contemporary economics textbooks.

4. Lockean political theory is an important force in shaping liberalism. In his *Treatise on Government* (1689), Locke argued against the doctrine of the divine right of kings and set up the natural right doctrine in political philosophy. The Lockean "natural right of life, liberty, and property" was derived from the right of labor to its own product. Thus, John R. Commons says, "John Locke united Law, Economics, and Ethics in a single concept of labor."[15] This is one of the plausible explanations for the tenacity with which Adam Smith and David Ricardo clung to the labor theory of value. It is also why Gunnar Myrdal named his well-known book, *The Political Element in the Development of Economic Theory.*[16]

5. John Locke's specific contribution to economics is in monetary theory. In *Some Considerations of the Consequences of Lowering the Interest and Raising the Value of Money* (1691), Locke gave the first clear formulation of the quantity theory of money. From the time of Jean Bodin (1530–96), many mercantilists held one or another simple version of the quantity theory. As Jacob Viner points out, however, "in most cases they failed to incorporate it as an integral part of their foreign-trade doctrine and failed also to show any concern about its consistency with the rest of their doctrine."[17] Locke made some advance in incorporating the quantity theory into the foreign trade doctrine, but a satisfactory synthesis occurred only later in David Hume's famous "price-specie flow mechanism," which became the foundation of the classical theory of the balance-of-payments adjustment process.[18] In discussing the effect of an increase in the quantity of money on the general price level, Locke did not consider the dynamics of the transmission mechanism involved in that process. What is the transmission mechanism? The answer is provided by Don Patinkin in his seminal book, *Money, Interest, and Prices,* as follows:

The most persuasive formulations of this theory were developments of the following tripartite thesis: an increase in the quantity of money disturbs the optimal relation between the level of money balances and the individual's expenditures; the disturbance generates an increase in the planned volume of these expenditures (the real-balance effect); and this increase creates pressures on the price level which push it upwards until it has risen in the same proportion as the quantity on money.[19]

What Locke missed is the transmission mechanism of a change in the monetary impulse, that is, the disturbance generates a change in the money holder's planned expenditures. Thus, Locke unwittingly committed the sin of the "homogeneity postulate." However, he was in good company. For, according to Patinkin, there is a missing chapter in the writings of Walras, Marshall, and Pigou as well: "Only Wicksell and Fisher provide complete, systematic statements of the tripartite thesis."[20]

6. It was the works of John Locke that popularized Newton's mechanistic world view among the French intelligentsia of the eighteenth century. The most famous of the French true believers was the "laughing philosopher," François Marie Arouet (1694–1778), better known as Voltaire. In *English Letters* (1773), Voltaire wrote:

as you are desirous to be informed of the great men England has produced, I shall begin with the Bacons, the Lockes and the Newtons. The generals and ministers will come after them in their turn.[21]

Voltaire was a great admirer of the English political and economic institutions. His sarcasm and criticisms against the Church and the state greatly undermined the existing regime. Some writers have said that Voltaire contributed one half of the French Revolution. The anticlerical atmosphere in France during the Enlightenment has been explained by Will Durant:

The failure of the Reformation to capture France had left for the Frenchmen no half-way house between infallibility and infidelity;

and while the intellect of Germany and England moved leisurely in the lines of religious evolution, the mind of France leaped from the hot faith which had massacred the Huguenots to cold hostility with which La Mettrie, Helvetius, Holbach, and Diderot turned upon the religion of their fathers.[22]

It is no exaggeration to say that Newton and Locke were the real founders of the Enlightenment. The leading ideas of the Enlightenment are: that the universe is a machine governed by inflexible laws—the laws of science, of politics, of economics, and of morality—that man cannot override; the "new natural law" can be discovered by reason and liberty; thus, a "new certainty" prevails and economics, philosophy, and physics are once more interrelated. All inner conflicts had been removed.

The Newtonian Heritage of Contemporary Economics

The implicit and explicit Newtonian assumptions still lurk behind contemporary economic models. In this section we attempt to pinpoint the hidden Newtonian assumptions in some of the current economic models.

Reductionism

An outstanding example of reductionist methodology is the derivation of the competitive market demand curve for a commodity, say commodity X. The market demand curve for X is the summation of individual demand curves for commodity X (the whole is equal to the sum of its parts). Figure 1.3 is a graphical representation of this reductionist approach.

The top part of Figure 1.3 is the familiar static constrained optimization of a consumer, i. The consumer with given tastes depicted by the iso-utility map (or indifference curves map), given the budget indicated by symbol I, facing the given commodities X and Y, rationally attempts to choose the optimal bundle of X and Y with the objective of maximizing his utility

Figure 1.3. **The derivation of Marshallian demand curve for commodity X from the constrained utility maximization of an individual**

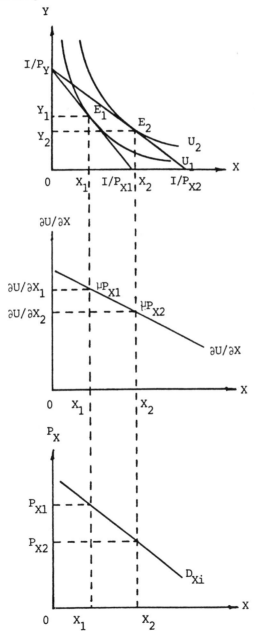

function, which is represented by equation (1), $U = U(X, Y)$. His budget constraint is described by equation (2), $I = P_xX + P_yY$. The Lagrangian expression is stated by equation (3), $Z = U + \mu(I - P_xX - P_yY)$, which combines the utility function and the budget constraint in an augmented new equation. The Greek mu (μ) is the Lagrange multiplier. The purpose of using the Lagrange-multiplier method is to convert a constrained maximization problem into a form such that the first-order condition of the free-extremum problem can still be applied. The economic meaning of μ is found to be the marginal utility of money income, which is represented by equation (11) in the following summary of mathematical statements.

The middle and bottom portions of Figure 1.3 illustrate the relationship between the marginal utility of money income and the individual demand curve for X. The mathematical statements of the derivation of the individual demand curve for commodity X are summarized as follows:

(1) the objective function:

$$U = U(X, Y)$$

(2) the budget constraint:

$$I = P_xX + P_yY$$

(3) the Lagrangian expression:

$$Z = U + \mu(I - P_xX - P_yY)$$

(4) $\qquad \delta Z/\delta X = 0 = \delta U/\delta X - \mu P_x$

(5) $\qquad \mu P_x = \delta U/\delta X$

(6) $\qquad \mu = (\delta U/\delta X)/P_x$

(7) $\qquad \delta Z/\delta Y = 0 = \delta U/\delta Y - \mu P_y$

$$(8) \qquad\qquad \mu P_y = \delta U/\delta Y$$

$$(9) \qquad\qquad \mu = (\delta U/\delta Y)/P_y$$

$$(10) \qquad\qquad \delta Z/\delta\mu = 0 = I - P_x X - P_y Y$$

$$(11) \qquad \mu = (\delta U/\delta X)/P_x = (\delta U/\delta X)/(\delta I/\delta X) = \delta U/\delta I.$$

The individual commodity X is expressed symbolically by D_{xi}. The downward sloping individual demand curve is based on the crucial Marshallian condition that the marginal utility of money income (μ) remains constant. If this condition is met, the relationship between the diminishing marginal utility of commodity X and the individual demand curve will be brought forth in bold relief.

The summation of all the individual demand curves for X will derive the market curve for X. This is reductionism par excellence. The whole can be reduced to its parts; the sum of its parts is equal to the whole.

Linearity

The assumption of linearity permeates the orthodox neoclassical economics. The following words of a true believer of neoclassical theory, Charles E. Ferguson, inadvertently lend support to this assertion:

> Neoclassical theory is a beautiful edifice erected upon the microeconomic production functions (and input-output pricing processes). If these production functions, and the aggregate production derived from them, possess certain characteristics [*linearly homogeneous*], the central results of neoclassical theory are obtained and the theory of production and distribution is validated. That is, if certain production relations hold, one may prove that the permanently sustainable consumption stream varies inversely with the rate of interest and that

Figure 1.4. **A schematic explanation of the effect of the linearly homogeneous production function on unified neoclassical theory**

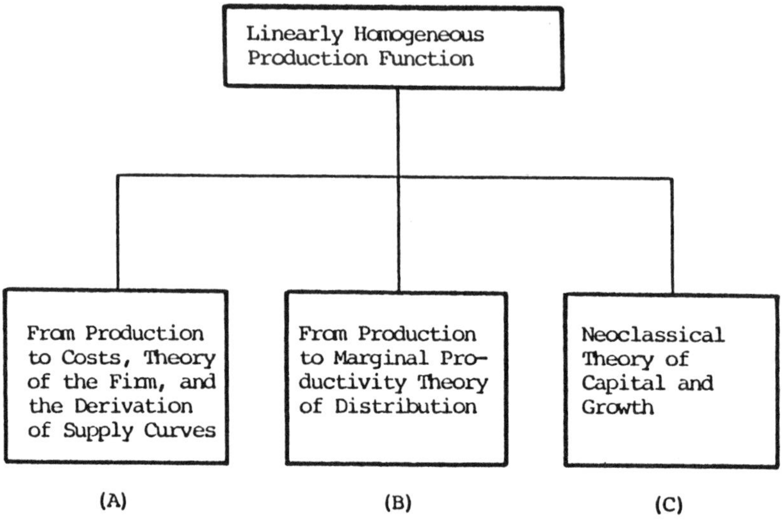

the maximum sustainable consumption per capita is attained when the rate of growth equals the rate of interest (or capital rent).[23]

In other words, once the linearly homogeneous production function is introduced into the unified neoclassical theory, one can derive (a) the theory of production costs which leads to the theory of the firm and the supply curves; (b) the marginal productivity theory of distribution; and (c) the derivative theory of capital and growth. Figure 1.4 is a schematic explanation of this proposition.

Figure 1.5 is a graphical demonstration of the Figure 1.4(A). The top part of Figure 1.5 is a micro-homogeneous production function, where capital $(\bar{K})$ is the fixed factor. When the fixed factor increases from K_1 to K_2, the production function shifts upwards. When the fixed factor increases again from K_2 to K_3, the production function makes another upward shift. The neoclassical production function depicts the law of variable factor

Figure 1.5. **From production to costs and leading toward individual firm's supply curves**

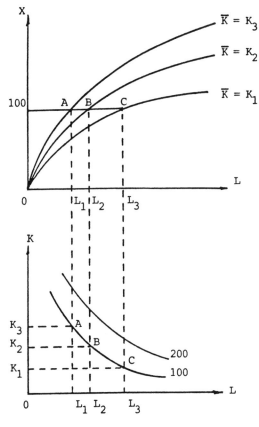

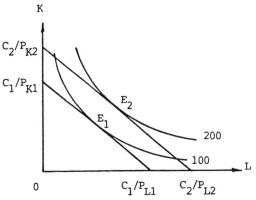

proportions. That is, there are different techniques available to produce the same output. For example, if the producer decides to produce output X at the level of 100 units, he can choose the capital-intensive technique A, or he can choose a labor-intensive technique such as C. It is the relative input prices (P_K/P_L) that guide him to pick the cost-saving technique. The middle portion of Figure 1.5 depicts the derivation of equal product curve (or iso-quant). It shows that the iso-quant of 100 units can be produced by any one of the three available techniques, namely, A, B, and C. An iso-quant map can be derived by increasing the output levels. The bottom of Figure 1.5 is the familiar diagram showing the firm's attempt to attain the so-called "least-cost-combination of inputs" under its budget constraint, which is analogous to the consumer's budget line. The constraint is sometimes called the "iso-cost line." By symmetrical reasoning, the tangent points E_1 and E_2 indicate the static constrained optimal choices of the firm. The total-cost curve (TC) can then be derived. The objective from production to costs is finally accomplished.

The total-cost approach could be changed to the average (or per-unit) costs approach. Using the U-shaped ATC, AVC, and MC curves, one can illustrate the profit-maximizing or loss-minimizing positions of the firm graphically.

We turn now to the marginal productivity theory of distribution as stated in Figure 1.4(B); this celebrated theory is another illustration of the Newtonian linearity assumption. The simplest way to explain the theory is to invoke the Cobb-Douglas production function, which, like the neoclassical production function, is also linearly homogeneous. The following equation (1) is the Cobb-Douglas production function:

(1) $$Y = K^{\alpha}L^{(1-\alpha)}$$

where Y stands for aggregate income; the α denotes the relative income share of owners of capital, which is derived by differentiating equation (1) partially with respect to capital, K:

(2) $\qquad \delta Y/\delta K = \alpha K^{\alpha-1}L^{1-\alpha} = \alpha K^{\alpha}L^{1-\alpha}/K = \alpha Y/K.$

Rearranging terms, one obtains the economic meaning of the symbol α:

(3) $\qquad \alpha = (\delta Y/\delta K)\cdot K/Y = MP_K\cdot K/Y.$

The economic meaning of the symbol $(1 - \alpha)$ is derived in the same way:

(4) $\quad \delta Y/\delta L = (1 - \alpha)L^{-\alpha}K^{\alpha} = (1 - \alpha)L^{1-\alpha}K^{\alpha}/L = (1 - \alpha)Y/L$

(5) $\qquad (1 - \alpha)Y = (\delta Y/\delta L)\cdot L = MP_L\cdot L$

(6) $\qquad (1 - \alpha) = (\delta Y/\delta L)\cdot L/Y,$ or,

(7) $\qquad (1 - \alpha) = MP_L\cdot L/Y.$

The linearity assumption is made explicit by the following:

(8) $\qquad \alpha + (1 - \alpha) = 1.$

By substituting equations (3) and (7) for α and $(1 - \alpha)$ in equation (8), the marginal productivity theory of distribution is established:

(9) $\qquad (\delta Y/\delta K\cdot K)/Y + (\mu Y/\delta L\cdot L)/Y = 1$

(10) $\qquad Y[(\delta Y/\delta K)\cdot K/Y] + Y[(\delta Y/\delta L)\cdot L/Y] = Y$

(11) $\qquad Y = (\delta Y/\delta K)\cdot K + (\delta Y/\delta L)\cdot L,$ or,

(12) $\qquad Y = MR_K\cdot K + MP_L\cdot L.$

The whole (Y) is simply the sum of its parts $(MP_K\cdot K$ and $MP_L\cdot L)$.

Figure 1.4(C) is concerned with the derivative theory of capital and growth. Charles E. Ferguson's "basic model in its simplest detail"[24] provides us with the clearest explanation:

Assume that there exists a production function

(1) $$Q = F(K, L)$$

that is homogeneous of degree one in single homogeneous real capital good (K) and homogeneous labor (L). By its homogeneity property, the production function may be written so as to relate the average product of labor $(y = Q/L)$ to the capital-labor ratio $(k = K/L)$:

(2) $$y = f(k).$$

Competitive imputation and linear homogeneity jointly imply that the wage rate (w) and the rate of return on capital or the rate of interest (r) may be written as:

(3) $$w = f(k) - kf'(k)$$

(4) $$r = f'(k).$$

Equations (2), (3), and (4) from the above quotation may be explained by Figure 1.6, which is not in Ferguson's seminal text.

With regard to the derived neoclassical growth theory, the linearly homogeneous production function has become the standard property of most models. The prototype of the basic neoclassical growth models may be written as follows:

(1) $$\dot{K} = sY,$$

which simply states the output-market equilibrium condition, namely, the equality of desired investment $(I = \dot{K})$ and desired saving $(S = sY)$.

(2) $$L = L_0 e^{nt}.$$

Figure 1.6. **From linearly homogeneous production function to marginal productivity theory of distribution. (A) shows that the equilibrium rate of return to capital in a competitive market is equal to the marginal product of capital (in per capita terms): $r = f'(k)$. (B) depicts that the total product, $y = Y/L$ is exhausted by factor payments no more, no less: $y = rk + wL$.**

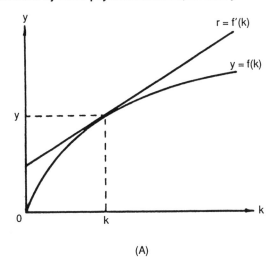

(A)

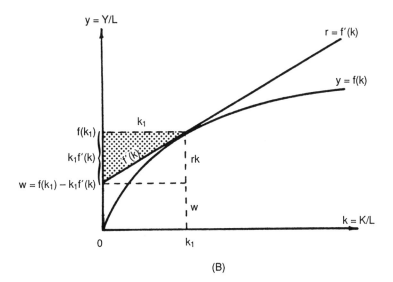

(B)

Equation (2) states that the exogenously determined constant growth rate of labor force is (n) percent per annum.

$$(3) \qquad\qquad Y = F(K,L).$$

The linearly homogeneous production function is introduced by equation (3).

By substituting equations (2) and (3) into (1), we obtain:

$$(4) \qquad\qquad \dot{K} = sF(K,L_o e^{nt}).$$

This equation expresses the time-path that capital accumulation must follow if the growing labor force is to remain fully employed.

$$(5) \qquad\qquad K = kL.$$

Equation (5) is simply another way of writing the definitional equation of capital-labor ratio. Substituting equation (2) into (5), we get:

$$(6) \qquad\qquad K = kL_o e^{nt}.$$

Differentiating equation (6) with respect to time, denoted by the symbol, t, yields:

$$(7) \qquad\qquad \dot{K} = knL_o e^{nt} + \dot{k}L_o e^{nt}.$$

Substituting equation (4) into (7) produces the following equation:

$$(8) \qquad\qquad sF(K, L_o e^{nt}) = knL_o e^{nt} + \dot{k}L_o e^{nt}.$$

Next, both sides of equation (8) are divided by the expression $L_o e^{nt}$ to produce:

(9) $sF(K/L_o e^{nt}, 1) = nk + \dot{k}.$

The fundamental equation of the basic model is derived by re-writing equation (9) as:

(10) $\dot{k} = sf(k) - nk$

which is a differential equation expressed in a single variable, k. It has two parameters, s and n. Figure 1.7 is a graphical representation of the fundamental equation: In this figure, we have:

$$sf(k) = nk,$$

$$sf(k)/k = n,$$

$$sy/k = n,$$

$$y/k = 1/\beta, \text{ and}$$

$s/\beta = n$ (Harrodian "Golden Age" growth rate) and $\dot{k} = 0$.

The diagram is the same as that of Figure 1.6. The new features are the nk line and the saving function, $sf(k)$, in per capita terms. One may call the nk line the "golden age" line, for it is the locus of all possible "golden age" points, or, "$sf(k) = nk$" points. It is analogous to the 45-degree line in the static Keynesian-cross diagram. "Golden age" growth rate of output means:

$$\dot{Y}/Y = \dot{K}/K = s/\beta = \dot{L}/L = n.$$

Capital accumulation, $\dot{k}$, depends upon the difference between $sf(k)$ and nk. If $sf(k)$ is greater than nk, $\dot{k} > 0$ and vice versa; $\dot{k}$ will be equal to zero if, and only if, $sf(k)$ equals nk. This equality is assured by the neoclassical assumption of competitive markets and flexible prices (including factor prices).[25]

Another illustration of the explicit assumption of linearity is

Figure 1.7. **From a linearly homogeneous production function, one can also obtain the derivative neoclassical growth theory. The Golden Age growth rate [sf (k) = nk] is assured by the neoclassical assumption of competitive markets and flexible prices.**

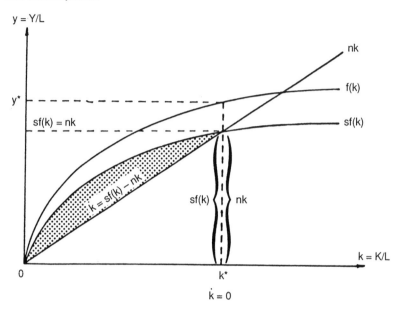

Paul A. Samuelson's "correspondence principle." Stability analysis began with Leon Walras, who presented the first formulation of the stability of competitive equilibrium for a two-commodity economy. The Walrasian equilibrium condition is that a price reduction (or increase) should increase excess demands (supplies). The Walrasian stability analysis was extended by John Hicks in 1939. In *Value and Capital* (which ushered in the so-called "Hicksian Revolution"), Hicks reformulated stability analysis for a multiple-commodity exchange economy.[26] His method was essentially that of comparative statics.

Samuelson suggested a new approach to the problem and laid the foundation of modern stability analysis in *Foundations of Economic Analysis* (1948). He introduced the "correspondence principle" and led stability analysis into the realm of dynamics. In explaining the common assumption that "if at any price demand exceeds supply, price will rise; if supply exceeds demand, price will fall,'' Samuelson wrote the following differential equation:

$$\dot{p} = dp/dt = H(q^d - q^s) = H[D(p, \Sigma) - S(p)]$$

where $q^d = D\ (p, \Sigma)$ which denotes the demand function. The letter Σ represents a shift parameter. $q^s = S(P)$ represents the supply function. $H(0) = 0$ and $H' > 0$. Samuelson then suggested that the stability properties of the differential equation could be found by taking the linear terms of the Taylor expansion of the right-hand side of the differential equation about the equilibrium point, p^0.[27] Samuelson writes:

> In the neighborhood of the equilibrium point, this can be expanded in the form
> $$\dot{p} = \mu\ (Dp^0 - Sp^0)(p - p^0) + \ldots$$
>
> If the equilibrium is to be stable,
> $$\lim_{t \to \infty} p(t) = p^0$$
>
> This is possible if, and only if,
> $$Dp^0 - Sp^0 \leq 0.$$
>
> If we rule out neutral equilibrium in the large and in the small, the equality sign may be omitted so that $Dp^0 - Sp^0 < 0$. If the supply curve is positively inclined, this will be realized. If it is negatively inclined, it must be less steep than the demand curve. If our stability conditions are realized, the problem originally proposed is answered. Price must rise when demand increases.[28]

Deterministic Prediction and Newtonian Absolute Time

For an age reared on Newtonian mechanics, it was only natural that determinism should become an implicit assumption for the classical economists, such as Adam Smith and David Ricardo. Karl Marx's prediction of the "inevitability of socialism" was no exception. Classical economists and Marxists alike failed to see what Robert L. Heilbroner called "the coexistence of freedom and necessity in history."[29] By "freedom" Heilbroner calls attention to the fact that there is openness in history; by "necessity" he refers to "the simultaneous existence of historical 'laws.' "

In spite of the marches of ambiguous events and disillusions during the three centuries since the Enlightenment, one can still detect the hold of the implicit assumption of deterministic predictability in some of our well-known contemporary economic models. In this section, two economic models will be considered as illustrations of this assertion.

The first is a model concerning the establishment of sufficient conditions under which market price adjustment mechanisms, of the Walrasian tatonnement variety, would be globally stable. The most lucid statement of this difficult model is the formulation of E. Roy Weintraub[30]:

Recall that, in general, the tatonnement can be written as

(1) $$\dot{P} = E(P)$$

where P is a column n-vector of prices, the state variables, and $E(P)$ is the column vector of the n excess demand functions.

Suppose that $(P^*) > 0$ is the (assumed) equilibrium vector, and consider the Lyapounov function

(2) $$\dot{V}(P) = 1/2 \sum_{i=1}^{n} (P_i - P_i^*)^2$$

Certainly $V(P)$ is always non-negative, zero only at equilibrium, and is continuously differentiable. . . . We find

(3) $$\dot{V}(P) = \sum_{i=1}^{n} (P_i - P_i^*)\dot{P}_i$$

substituting from (1),

(4)
$$\dot{V}(P) = \sum_{i=1}^{n} (P_i - P_i{}^*)E_i(P), \text{ or}$$

(5)
$$\dot{V}(P) = \sum_{i=1}^{n} P_i E_i(P) - \sum_{i=1}^{n} P_i{}^* E_i(P).$$

If Walras' Law holds, $\Sigma P_i E(P_i) = 0$ so we are left with the statement that

(6) $\Sigma P_i{}^* E_i(P) > 0$ implies (1) is stable.

Following Michael D. Intriligator,[31] the expression $V(P)$ can be interpreted as a measure of the distance between the disequilibrium prices and the equilibrium prices within the open region around the equilibrium prices (since we are talking about global stability here). Weintraub's equation (6) quoted above means that the distance falls over time, so global stability is eventually attained. The inward direction of $V(P)$ is depicted by Figure 1.8, in which at the point P^*, $V(P) = 0$.

The technical details of convergence of the neo-Walrasian stability analysis are indeed elegant. The Lyapounov method used, however, seems implicitly to assume Newtonian absolute time and deterministic predictability. In the opinion of Franklin M. Fisher, one overriding fact is far more important than the technical details of convertibility, and that is the "hysteresis effect" or "path dependence effect." According to Fisher, in the course of converging to equilibrium, traders' endowments change, and this inevitably changes the set of equilibria for the traders. In other words, the set of equilibria depends not only on the initial state but also on the dynamic adjustment process. This is the meaning of the "path dependence effect."[32]

The second model we will consider here is the optimal neoclassical growth model with an implicit Newtonian absolute time assumption. It has been recognized that this model is part of dynamic normative economics. It involves the choosing of the

Figure 1.8. **The Lyapounov function**

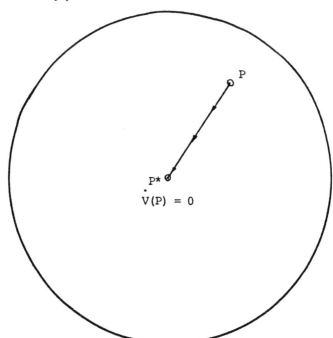

optimal time paths of some strategic variables, which will best satisfy some social objective. Hence, it is essentially a planning problem. As such, the neoclassical model is no longer objectionable to critics, since it is well known that the theory of perfectly competitive capitalism is equivalent in many respects to the theory of planned socialist economy.[33] The late Joan Robinson wrote:

> [t]here is one point on which I agree with [Robert M. Solow]—that the notion of factor allocation in conditions of perfect competition makes sense in a normative theory for a planned economy rather than in a descriptive theory for a capitalist economy, and that the notion of marginal productivity of investment makes sense in the context of socialist planning.[34]

The model under consideration is a simple optimal neoclassical model whose solutions are arrived at by invoking the Pontryagin maximum principle. The maximum principle may be regarded as an extension of the method of Lagrange multipliers used in static constrained optimization theory to dynamic constrained optimization problems. The optimal control problem of the simple model may be described as:

$$(1) \qquad y = f(k) = c + nk + \dot{k},$$

where y stands for output per man; c denotes per capita consumption; nk represents capital widening; and k signifies net investment of capital accumulation. Equation (1) describes an economic system at a point in time. It states the allocation of scarce resources (y) among three competing uses (c, nk, and k). The objective of the central planning board is supposed to be the raising of the standard of living of the people, as measured by per capita consumption (c). Assume that the central planning board has a utility function expressing utility as a function of consumption per man:

$$(2) \qquad U = U(c), U'(c) > 0, U''(c) < 0.$$

The dynamic constrained optimization problem in the present case is that of choosing the optimal time path of c from a given class of time paths, $c(t)$, over the relevant planning period with a view to maximizing the social welfare function, denoted by W. The starting date of the planning period is symbolized by t_0; the terminal date of the planning period is denoted by t_T. The time path $c(t)$ is called the control variable. The identity equation of per capita consumption is derived by rearranging the terms of equation (1):

$$(3) \qquad c = f(k) - nk - \dot{k}.$$

When we look at equation (3), it is obvious that $\dot{k}$ is a constraining factor for c. k is called the state variable which describes the economic system at a point in time. (It is analogous to the chief

of state's "state of the union" speech.) The equation of motion
for k is obtained by rearranging the terms of equation (3):

(4) $$\dot{k} = f(k) - nk - c.$$

The objective functional (in the context of calculus of variations, not calculus as in the static case) of the planners to be
maximized by the chosen optimal $c(t)$ is:

(5) $$max\ W = \int_{t_0}^{T} U(c)dt = \int_{t_0}^{T} Fdt = \int_{t_0}^{T} U[f(k) - nk - \dot{k}]dt.$$

W is obtained by integrating all instantaneous contributions to
total utility by consumption per man over the relevant planning
period. F is sometimes referred to as the "performance curve"; it
is the same as $U[f(k) - nk - k]$. This expression is derived simply
by substituting equation (3) into equation (2). The concepts of
choosing the optimal "performance curve," $k(t)$, and the constrained maximization of the objective functional, as well as the
two constraints (i.e., the boundary conditions—the capital stock
at the starting period, k_0 and that of the terminal period, k_T,) are
depicted by Figure 1.9, in which the optimal performance curve
is F_2^* and the shaded area under F_2^* is the maximand. The other
feasible trajectories are indicated by F_1 and F_3 in the control set.

Following the Pontryagin maximum principle, a Hamiltonian
equation (which is analogous to the static constrained optimization problem) is introduced. The Hamiltonian is a Lagrangian
expression that is written as:

(6) $H(c, k, \mu) = U(c) + \mu\dot{k} = U[f(k) - nk - \dot{k}] + \mu[f(k) - nk - c]$

Equation (6) is a Legendre transformation of equation (5) into an
equivalent form after introducing a new variable, μ, the dynamic
Lagrange multiplier. It should be noted that the Hamiltonian is
the sum of three elements: (a) the integrand of the objective

Figure 1.9. **The optimal "performance curve" is shown as F_2^*. Other feasible, but not optimal, trajectories are indicated by F^1 and F^3 in the control set. F_2^* is optimal because the shaded area under it is the maximand.**

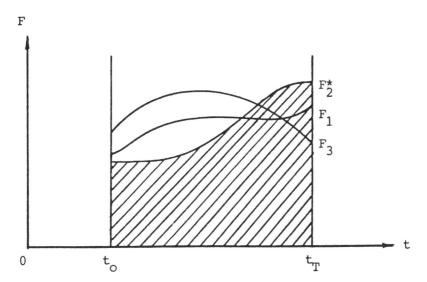

functional, namely, $U(c)$; (b) the costate variable, μ, and (c) the constraint, k. The reason why μ is called the costate variable is that each μ corresponds to one of the differential equations of motion. Thus, μ varies over the time together with k. Furthermore, the Hamiltonian may be considered as total output measured in terms of per capita utility, $U(c)$. This is because the two components of the total output are: (a) the utility of the consumption flow, $U(c)$, and (b) the marginal utility lost from additional capital formation (given the scarce resource at any point in time, y, an increase in the allocation of y to k necessarily means a decrease in the resources available for c). Thus, μ may be viewed as the "shadow price" of capital accumulation ($\dot{k}$). This point is clarified below.

To find the optimal $c(t)$ that maximizes the Hamiltonian, four maximum conditions should be satisfied. *The first maximum condition* involves differentiating equation (6) with respect to c and setting the partial expression, $\delta H/\delta c$, equal to zero (the first-order condition), to obtain:

(7) $$\delta H/\delta c = 0 = \delta[U(c)]/\delta c + \delta[\mu\dot{k}]/\delta c$$

(8) $$0 = U'(c) + \mu\cdot\delta[f(k) - nk - c]/\delta c$$

(9) $$0 = U'(c) - \mu$$

(10) $\mu = U'(c)$ implies that μ can be interpreted as the marginal utility of per capita consumption, $U'(c)$.

The second maximum condition involves the employment of the Euler-Lagrange equation of calculus of variations, which may be written as:

(11) $$\delta F/\delta k = d(\delta F/\delta \dot{k})/dt.$$

Let us look at the right-hand side of equation (11) first. Keeping $\dot{k}$ constant, F is partially differentiated with respect to k:

(12) $$\delta F/\delta k = \delta\{U[f(k) - nk - \dot{k}]\}/\delta k \text{ yields:}$$

(13) $$\delta F/\delta k = [f'(k) - n]\cdot U'.$$

Turning to the left-hand side of the equation, keeping k constant, we may differentiate F partially with respect to $\dot{k}$:

(14) $$\delta F/\delta \dot{k} = \delta\{U[f(k) - nk - \dot{k}]\}/\delta \dot{k} \text{ yields:}$$

(15) $$\delta F/\delta \dot{k} = U'\cdot(-1).$$

Now, $\delta F/\delta \dot{k}$ is partially differentiated with respect to time, t:

(16) $$d(\delta F/\delta k)/dt = -\dot{U}'.$$

Substituting equations (13) and (16) into equation (11) produces:

(17) $$\dot{U}'/U' = -[f'(k) - n].$$

Since $\mu = U'(c) = U'$, equation (17) may be rewritten as:

$$(18) \qquad \dot{\mu}/\mu = -[f'(k) - n].$$

The third maximum condition involves the derivation of the optimal $\dot{c}$ by means of equation (18). This derivation is as follows:

$$(19) \qquad U' = U'(c)$$

$$(20) \qquad \dot{U}' = U''(c)\dot{c}$$

$$(21) \qquad \dot{U}'/= U' \, [U''(c)/U']\dot{c}$$

$$(22) \qquad \text{Let } \tau = -(dU'/U')/(dc/c) = -(dU'/dc)\cdot(c/U')$$

$$(23) \qquad \tau = -U''(c)\cdot c/U' = -U''[(c)/U']c$$

$$(24) \qquad -\tau/c = U''(c)/U'.$$

Substituting this expression into equation (21), we obtain:

$$(25) \qquad \dot{U}'/U' = -(\tau/c)\cdot\dot{c}.$$

Substituting equation (17) into equation (25) yields:

$$(26) \qquad -[f'(k) - n] = -(\tau/c)\dot{c}$$

$$(27) \qquad \dot{c} = c[f'(k) - n]/\tau.$$

If $f'(k) = n$, both the steady-state c and k will be obtained:

$$(28) \qquad \dot{c} = 0; \; \dot{k} = 0; \text{ and } f(k) = nk + c.$$

Figure 1.10 depicts the process of optimization.

To obtain $H = 0$ is *the fourth and last maximum condition*. To read this objective, one has, first of all, to derive the following two canonical equations of the model under consideration:

Figure 1.10. **Depiction of the optimization process of a simple neoclassical growth model. The optimal trajectory of per capita consumption, C, is obtained when f'(k) = n.**

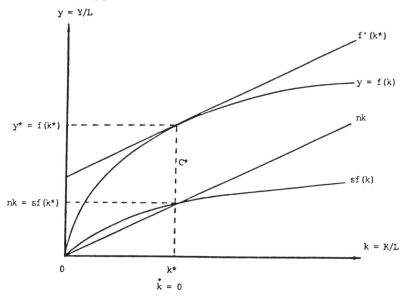

(29) $$\delta H/\delta k = \delta\{U[f(k) - nk - \dot{k}]\}/\delta k + \delta(\mu\dot{k})/\delta k$$
$$= [f'(k) - n]\cdot U' + 0.$$

Rearranging terms, we get:

(30) $$\delta H/\delta k = -\dot{\mu}.$$

This is one of the canonical equations. The other one is derived as follows:

(31) $$\delta H/\delta\mu = \delta[U(c)]/\delta\mu + \delta[\mu\dot{k}]/\delta\mu = \dot{k}.$$

Now, we can proceed to attain the objective, $H = 0$:

(32) $$\dot{H} = dH/dt = U'(c)\dot{c} + \mu\dot{k} + \dot{k}\mu.$$

Since $\mu = U'(c)$ and $\dot{\mu} = -\mu[f(k) - n]$, equation (32) can be rewritten as:

(33) $$\dot{H} = \mu\dot{c} + \mu\ddot{k} + \dot{k}\{-\mu[f'(k) - n]\}$$

(34) $$\dot{H} = \mu\dot{c} + \mu\ddot{k} - \mu f'(k)\dot{k} + \mu n\dot{k}$$

(35) $$\ddot{k} = d[f(k) - nk - c]/dt = f'(k)\dot{k} - n\dot{k} - \dot{c}$$

(36) $$\mu\ddot{k} = \mu f'(k)\dot{k} - \mu n\dot{k} - \mu\dot{c}.$$

Substituting equation (36) into equation (34) yields:

(37) $$\dot{H} = \mu\dot{c} + \mu f'(k)\dot{k} - \mu n\dot{k} - \mu\dot{c} - \mu f'(k)\dot{k} + \mu n\dot{k}.$$

The right-hand side terms cancel one another out. Therefore:

(38) $$\dot{H} = 0$$

With much ado the central planners have finally hit the bull's eye. There is deterministic predictability. Time has neither any role nor any dimension in this dynamic process. There is no "hysteresis effect," only "tunnel vision" and unwarranted optimism (only "necessity" in history).

The firm grip of the "Laplacian demon" on this model is not surprising. For the fundamental principle of classical dynamics as reformulated by William Rowen Hamilton (1805–65) is a dynamic analog of the static Lagrangian multiplier method which shows that nearly all gravitational, optical, dynamical, and electrical laws can be explained by a maximizing or minimizing process. In Hamilton's hands, all the properties of classical dynamics are summarized in terms of a single function, the Hamiltonian, H. The actual motion of a dynamic system in the interval from a given initial position to a given final terminal position is such that for this motion the integral is stationary.

Originally the Hamiltonian function, H, described total energy as the sum of the system's potential energy and kinetic energy. Through the derivatives of the Hamiltonian, which describes the time variation of the coordinates and momenta, one obtains the canonical equations. "These canonical equations," observe Prigogine and Stengers, "contain the general properties of all dynamic changes. Here we have the triumph of the mathematization of nature. All dynamic change to which classical dynamics applies can be reduced to these simple mathematical equations."[35]

The application of the Hamiltonian principle in economics is illustrated by the optimal neoclassical model described in the preceding paragraphs. The Hamiltonian, H, is depicted by equation (6) where H is analogous to total energy, which is the sum of potential and kinetic energy. In the optimal growth model, the sum is represented by $H = U(c) + k$. The analogy between kinetic energy and the equation of motion $k = f(k) - nk - c$ is apparent. The canonical equations in the model are depicted by equations (30), $\delta H/\delta k = \dot{\mu}$, and (31), $\delta H/\delta \mu = k$. The static character of the optimal trajectories is reflected in the derivation of the optimal equilibrium growth paths to the steady state: $c = 0$, $k = 0$, and $H = 0$.

Notes

1. Thomas S. Kuhn, *The Copernican Revolution* (New York: Vintage Books, Random House, 1957), p. 1.

2. David Bohm, *Wholeness and the Implicate Order* (London: Ark Paperbacks, 1983), p. 113.

3. Fritjof Capra, *The Turning Point* (New York: Bantam, 1982), p. 59.

4. Sir John Hicks, *Causality in Economics* (New York: Basic Books, 1979), p. 8.

5. K.R. Atkins, *Physics* (New York: John Wiley, 1965), p. 69.

6. Ibid., p. 76.

7. Ibid., p. 78.

8. Paul Davies, *The Cosmic Blueprint* (New York: Simon & Schuster, 1988), p. 10.

9. Edwin Burmeister and A. Rodney Dobell, *Mathematical Theories of Economics Growth* (London: Macmillan, 1970), p. 1.

10. Morris Kline, *Mathematics in Western Culture* (New York: Oxford University Press, 1964), p. 214.

11. Davies, *Cosmic Blueprint*, p. 14.

12. Nicholas Capaldi, ed., *The Enlightenment: The Proper Study of Mankind* (New York: Capricorn Books, 1968), p. 1.

13. Crane Brinton, *The Shaping of Modern Thought* (Englewood Cliffs, NJ: Prentice-Hall, 1950), p. 19.

14. Capaldi, *The Enlightenment*, p. 19.

15. John R. Commons, *Institutional Economics* (Madison: University of Wisconsin Press, 1961), p. 25.

16. Gunnar Myrdal, *The Political Element in the Development of Economic Theory* (New York: Simon & Schuster, 1954).

17. Jacob Viner, *Studies in the Theory of International Trade* (New York: Harper & Row, 1937), pp. 76–78.

18. Also see Joseph Aschheim and Ching-Yao Hsieh, *Macroeconomics: Income and Monetary Theory* (Washington, DC: University Press of America reprint, 1980), pp. 142–44.

19. Don Patinkin, *Money, Interest, and Prices*, 2nd ed. (New York: Harper & Row, 1965), pp. 163–64.

20. Ibid., p. 164.

21. Cited by Capaldi, *The Enlightenment*, p. 56.

22. Will Durant, *The Story of Philosophy* (New York: Simon & Schuster, 1953), p. 175.

23. Charles E. Ferguson, *The Neoclassical Theory of Production and Distribution* (Cambridge: Cambridge University Press, 1969), p. 12; "[*linearly homogeneous*]" has been added by us.

24. Ibid., p. 253.

25. For detailed explanations, see Ching-Yao Hsieh et al., *A Short Introduction to Modern Growth Theory* (Washington, DC: University Press of America, 1978), chaps. 1–4.

26. See John Hicks, *Value and Capital* (Oxford: Oxford University Press, 1939), chap. 5.

27. Paul A. Samuelson, *Foundations of Economic Analysis* (Cambridge, MA: Harvard University Press, 1948), p. 263.

28. Ibid., p. 263.

29. Robert L. Heilbroner, *The Future as History* (New York: Grove Press, 1959), p. 182.

30. E. Roy Weintraub, *Micro-Foundations: The Compatibility of Microeconomics and Macroeconomics* (London: Cambridge University Press, 1979), pp. 109–10.

31. Michael E. Intriligator, *Mathematical Optimization and Economic Theory* (Englewood Cliffs, NJ: Prentice-Hall, 1971).

32. See Franklin M. Fisher, *Disequilibrium Foundations of Equilibrium Economics* (New York: Cambridge University Press, 1983), p. 14.

33. See O. Lange and F. Taylor, *On the Economic Theory of Socialism* (Minneapolis: University of Minnesota Press, 1938), and E. Barone, "The Ministry of Production in the Collective State," in F.A. Hayek, ed., *Collective Economics Planning* (London: Routledge & Kegan Paul, 1935), pp. 247–90.

34. Joan Robinson, "Solow on the Rate of Return," in *Collected Economic Papers*, vol. 3 (Oxford: Blackwell, 1965). Reprinted in G.C. Harcourt and N.F. Laing, eds., *Capital and Growth* (Harmondsworth, UK: Penguin Modern Economics Readings, 1971), p. 168.

35. Ilya Prigogine and Isabelle Stengers, *Order out of Chaos* (New York: Bantam, 1984), p. 71.

Chapter 2

The Romantic Protest against the Newtonian Mechanistic World View

The first wave of revolutions against the eighteenth-century mechanistic world view was the Romantic movement. We should note that the Romantic movement was not a revolt against reason per se; rather, it was a revolt against the narrow, dogmatic rationalism of the Enlightenment. The lopsided glorification of reason had been satirized by a wit in the past as follows:

> God is reason, the Bible is Newtonian physics; and the prophet is Voltaire.

What was the quarrel between the romantics and the rationalists? Bruce Wilshire answers the question succinctly:

> The freedom of the individual is the theme common to both ages. . . .
> But at no time in history has individualism and the quest for freedom
> been more intense than the romantics. Their quarrel with the ratio-
> nalists of the Enlightenment broke out over the proper formulation of
> the theme of freedom.[1]

Another way to express this situation is that the romantics argued that the rationalists' approach, based on Cartesian reductionism and Newtonian mechanics, had created a "fragmented

41

man.'' What they wanted was the recovery of the ''whole man'' by way of what T.Z. Lavine calls ''the quest for the Totality of Experience.''[2]

The impact of this widespread movement on politics and the arts has been well documented in many contemporary texts. The purpose of this chapter is to consider the alternative approach of Romanticism to philosophy, science, and economics in the light of the central theme of our book.

Romanticism and Philosophy

The original inspiration for the Romantic alternative approach to philosophy was the German transcendental idealism of Immanuel Kant (1724–1804), whose seminal book, *Critique of Pure Reason* (1781), exposed the limitations of science and rationalism. According to Lavine, ''In order to save the truth of sciences, Kant has to make the laws of science dependent upon the mind and its concept.''[3]

Kant's emphasis is on the subjective and ideal, rather than the objective and real. This also means that Kant opened the flood gate for the subsequent romantics to believe almost anything they wanted to believe.

The Kantian twist lends support to the romantics' claim for the primacy of will. It also fortified their belief that nature is not a machine but is instead ''a living spirit, a vast will, and a wiser teacher than a scientific treatise.''[4] In the light of this background, one can understand why Arthur Schopenhauer (1788–1860) wrote his great anthology of pessimism, *The World as Will and Idea* (1818). One can also have a better understanding of George Whilhelm Hegel's assertion that history is a process of ''becoming''—the march of the spirit toward freedom.

The English Romantic poets firmly believed that nature is a living spirit and a wiser teacher than are scientists, and specifically physicists. In their unceasing quest for the recovery of the ''whole man,'' they prescribed communion with nature as the first step. This communion would arouse the spontaneous flow of powerful feeling. According to Bruce Wilshire,

> this is a key . . . to understanding the romantics: self-conscious man first finds himself beyond himself. He finds himself in nature pre-dominantly, but also in civilizations of the past and in possible ones of the future; for his knowledge of nature is a function of his learning, and his learning is a function of civilization.[5]

The romantics' love of nature led them to attack the hideousness of the industrial cities. H.G. Schenk tells us that "Although man had not yet embarked of building sky-scrapers, and the most populous cities contained fewer than a million inhabitants, the Romantics often compared them to great human deserts."[6] At the risk of oversimplicification, the view of the romantics may be summarized by Figure 2.1. Hegel's philosophy reflects the romantics' inclination to champion biology because the notion of "organism" provides them with a metaphor for much of their speculative thought.

Other Romantic philosophers and artists embraced the notion of organicism mentioned by Lavine:

> Kant viewed the a priori concepts and other structures of consciousness as an organic unity; Goethe viewed nature as an organic totality; the Romantic poets, Schlegel, Wordsworth, and Coleridge, all viewed true art as achieving organic unity out of multiplicity; social philosophers such as Rousseau, Herder, and Burke viewed society, not as an Enlightenment aggregate of atomic individuals, but as an organic unity.[7]

Historicism is another biological metaphor introduced by Hegel. According to Lavine:

> Historicism is the claim that the understanding of any aspect of human life must be concerned primarily with its history, its evolution, its genesis, or its roots, rather than with empirical observation of it as it is now. Historicism is the view that adequate knowledge of any human phenomenon must be historical.[8]

Figure 2.1. **A schematic representation of the mind of the romantics**

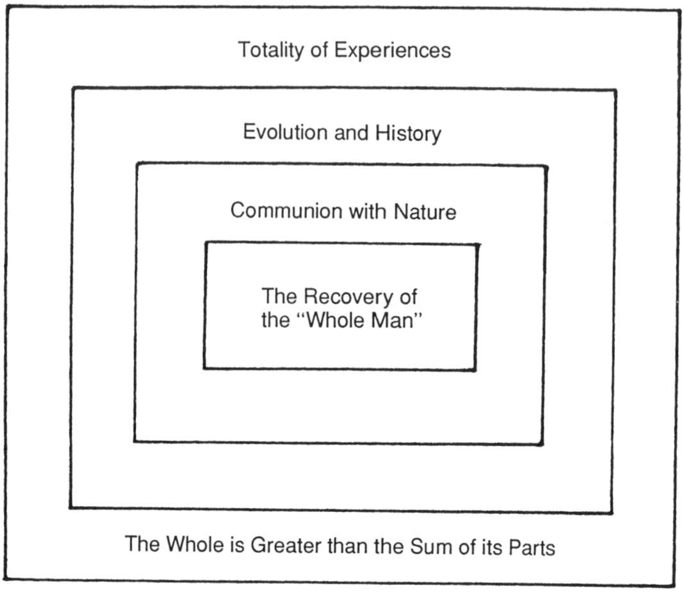

The romantics appear to have reached back to some aspects of the Aristotelian and Thomist organic view of nature. There is, however, at least one major difference between the two organic views: that is in the realm of feeling and emotion. The romantic glorifies passion, whereas Aristotle and St. Thomas, like the philosophers of the Enlightenment, worshiped reason.

Romanticism and Science

The Romantic movement flourished during the first half of the nineteenth century. It was a period of rapid changes. The Industrial Revolution was gaining momentum; medicine and the biological sciences underwent significant advances; and the population of Europe surged. José Ortega y Gasset calls this population growth "the coming of the masses."[9]

As already mentioned, the romantics embraced the organic

view of nature. Thus, they were inclined to reject Newtonian mechanics and to champion biology instead. However, they did not formulate any systematic scientific theory of organic evolution. Their theories of evolution were essentially philosophical. The only exception, perhaps, is the positivism of August Comte (1798–1857). The term "positivism" is associated with Comte for it was Comte who asserted that the only knowledge of any value is knowledge that comes from the sciences. It must be noted that the Comtean positivism differs from the logical positivism of the twentieth century. As Leszek Kolakowski points out, "his doctrine contains a particularly large number of elements looked upon as alien to currently accepted positivist preoccupations and even incompatible with them."[10]

The central idea of Comtean positivism is the law of three stages in the history of the evolution of human mind. Comte proclaimed that all the sciences pass through similar stages of development but not necessarily at the same speed. The first stage, the theological stage, according to Kolakowski, "covers mankind's progress from fetishism to polytheism and on to monotheism; it corresponds to the most primitive stage of social life-theocracy."[11] The second stage is the metaphysical stage. In this stage, the scientific constructs were based on observed facts, such as "forces," "qualities and quantities," and "properties." The third, or positive, stage of intellectual development correlates with the Age of the Enlightenment. In this stage, August Comte introduced his ideas of social reform, which are quite different from those of the philosophers of the Enlightenment. He rejected Lockean individualism. On the contrary, Comte embraced the view of society as an organic whole (here the tinge of Romanticism comes into the picture). Furthermore, Comte's view of the organic whole is also different from Aristotle and St. Thomas. The organic society of Comte must be based on science.

The Comtean methodology has been criticized by the contemporary neo-Austrian theorists, who call it "scientism in the study of man." Murray N. Rothbard asserts that:

> Scientism is the profoundly unscientific attempt to transfer uncritically the methodology of the physical sciences to the study of human action. Both fields of inquiry must, it is true, be studied by the use of reasons—the mind's identification of reality. But then it becomes crucially important, in reason, not to neglect the critical attribute of human action: that, alone in nature, human beings possess a rational consciousness. Stones, molecules, planets cannot choose their courses; their behavior is strictly and mechanically determined for them. To ignore this primordial fact about the nature of man—to ignore his volition, his free will—is to misconstrue the facts of reality and therefore to be profoundly and radically unscientific.[12]

It was Comte's vision that religion based on theological beliefs would be replaced in the future by a new religion of humanity and altruism. This positive religion will bring men together in a common devotion to social justice and benevolence. This was Comte's idea concerning social reform. Although he placed biology at the top of the hierarchy of sciences, he did not formulate any scientific biological theory. He died in 1859, just before the publication of Darwin's *Origin of Species*. He should, however, have been acquainted with the works of his contemporary, Jean Baptiste Lamarck (1744–1829). In 1809, Lamarck was the first to introduce a coherent hypothesis of organic evolution. He suggested that all living beings have evolved from earlier and simpler forms under the pressure of their environment. In other words, according to Lamarck, an animal will acquire new habits when it encounters environmental change. The acquired new habits will gradually lead to structural changes of the animal's body that may be transmitted to offspring. The inheritance of these structural changes will eventually produce a new species of the animal.

It must be noted that Lamarck's theory of inherited characteristics was the watershed of the development of the theory of organic evolution. Ever since antiquity, philosophers and theologians had entertained the idea that all living species were descending from God. The philosophers of the Enlightenment did not question this great chain of being. Lamarckian theory, however, challenged the idea of this chain.

Lamarck did not give a full account of evolution; he only touched one aspect of the theory of evolution, namely, inheritance. A more complete theory requires two other aspects: (a) Charles Darwin's theory of random mutation and natural selection, and (b) Gregor Mendel's genetics. Paul Davies observes that the spectacular advances in genetics and molecular biology in the modern era have reaffirmed the essential ideas of Darwinism. Today biologists can understand the mechanism of evolutionary change at the molecular level (e.g., an organism's DNA).[13]

These important advances in the biological sciences came after the heyday of the Romantic movement (the first half of the nineteenth century). This is probably an important explanation for the failure of historicism and scientism during the Romantic era to topple the Newtonian mechanical world view.

Furthermore, as Paul Davies points out: "Almost all modern biologists are mechanists, and the mechanistic paradigm is responsible for remarkable progress in understanding the nature of life. . . . One hears it said that biology is just a branch of chemistry, which is in turn just a branch of physics."[14]

Romanticism and Economics

"Organicism" and "historicism" dominated the economic writings of the thinkers of the Age of Romanticism. A firm believer in technical economics, Joseph A. Schumpeter held a very low opinion of the economic writings of that period. He wrote: "There are none to be recorded so far as technical economics is concerned."[15] He conceded, however, that the Romantic movement produced all kinds of historical research: "It taught us better understanding of civilizations other than our own—this meant new vistas, wider horizons, fresh problems, and above all, the end of the stupid contempt that Voltaireans and utilitarians professed for everything that preceded 'the enlightened age.' "[16] The founder of the Historical School was Wilhelm Georg

Friedrich Roscher (1817–94). Other representatives included Bruno Hildebrand (1812–78) and Karl Knies (1821–98), both of whom made no pretense of doing anything beyond a study of economic history.

The attack on the English classical political economy by the Historical School began during the second half of the nineteenth century. The political background was the Bismarck era. Otto von Bismarck spearheaded the movement toward the unification of Germany. The members of the younger German Historical School generally were under the spell of German nationalism. The main points of their criticisms against the classical and neoclassical schools are succinctly summarized by Homa Katouzian as follows:

> (a) Historical investigation should be the correct procedure for the study of economics. The classical economists adopted the wrong procedure of abstraction in formulating general hypothesis.
> (b) Historical investigation would in time lead to the formulation of "general laws" through the process of induction.
> (c) Such "general laws" are not universally applicable. They would be specific to certain stages of history. And
> (d) There can be differences in policy conclusions according to the various socio-cultural frameworks.[17]

The leader of the younger Historical School was Gustav von Schmoller (1838–1917). The four points stated in the preceding paragraph represent his view. In 1883, Carl Menger (1840–1921) published his second major work, *Problems of Economics and Sociology*, in which he attacked the historical approach to economics. Schmoller reacted swiftly in defense of his position. Thus was launched the *Methodenstreit*—the famous debate over method.

On the question of whether or not there are universal economic laws, Ben B. Seligman describes a witty encounter between Schmoller and Vilfredo Pareto (1848–1923):

> Once, when Gustav Schmoller challenged Pareto, saying that there were no economic laws, Pareto politely asked if there were any

restaurants where one might eat for nothing. Schmoller disdainfully replied that one always had to pay something. That, retorted Pareto, was natural economic law.[18]

During the height of the Romantic movement, the most outstanding antagonist of classical political economy was Jean Charles Leonard Simonde de Sismondi (1773–1842). The other antagonists were the "utopian socialists," such as the Count of Saint-Simon (1760–1825), Charles Fourier (1772–1837), Robert Owen (1771–1858), and Pierre-Joseph Proudhon (1809–65).

Sismondi was not a socialist, but his works have been much read and carefully studied by socialists. Karl Marx and Friedrich Engels, in the *Manifesto of the Communist Party*, call Sismondi's work "petty bourgeois socialism," yet they write:

> This school of socialism dissected with great acuteness the contradictions in the conditions of modern production. It laid bare the hypocritical apologies of economists. It proved, incontrovertibly, the disastrous effects of machinery and few hands, overproduction and crises; it pointed out the inevitable ruin of the petty bourgeois and peasants, the misery of the proletariate, the anarchy in production, the crying inequalities in the distribution of wealth, the industrial war of extermination between nations, the dissolution of old moral bonds, of the old family relationships, of the old nationalities.[19]

Sismondi has an underconsumption theory of crises. In spite of his low opinion of the writers of the Romantic movement, Schumpeter gives high marks to Sismondi. According to Schumpeter, "the distinctive feature of Sismondi's analysis is that it is geared to an explicit dynamic model in the modern sense of this phrase."[20] He goes on to state that:

> Sismondi's great merit is that he used, systematically and explicitly, a schema of periods, that is, that he was the first to practice the particular method of dynamics that is called period analysis. Moreover, he saw clearly the difference this makes and in particular the disturbances, discrepancies, and hitches that result from the fact that economic life is bound to sequences of which every unit is determined by the past and in turn determines the future.[21]

According to Michael Bleaney:

> it is right to point out the dynamic aspects of this analysis, for the usual formulation of ''Say's Law'' at this time runs purely in terms of comparative statics, with no indication of how the progress from one situation to the other was achieved. It is therefore a step forward to look closely at the relation between successive time-periods.[22]

Although some of the important social ideas in the nineteenth century can be traced back to Sismondi's writings, the most influential socialist thinker in the first half of the century is, unquestionably, Karl Heinrich Marx (1818–83). Marx was twenty-six years old when his *Economic and Philosophic Manuscripts* (1844) was translated into English. The far-reaching influence of Marx's manuscripts is pinpointed by Ivan Svitak:

> Even today any reference to Marx's *Economic and Philosophic Manuscripts* of 1844 arouses the interest of both orthodox and unorthodox. The gist of this work can be expressed as follows: *Communism without humanism is no communism and humanism without communism cannot be humanism.*[23]

The essence of Marxian Humanism is visually summarized by Figure 2.2, which represents a variation of the familiar ''production possibilities frontier.'' Consumer goods production is measured by the vertical axis; the production of investment goods is measured by the horizontal axis. The full employment of given resources, including science and technology in the production of the two types of goods and services, is depicted by the technology in the ''production possibilities curve.'' Marx rejected classical political economy and other ''false brothers'' of ''true socialism,'' such as crude egalitarian communism, utopian socialism, anarchism, and so forth, for all of them were toiling in the realm of necessity. None of them could cross the threshold of ''pre-human history.'' In the diagram, classical political economy and ''false brothers'' of ''true socialism'' are represented by points *A*, *B*, and *C* inside the ''production possibilities curve.''

Figure 2.2. **Marxian humanism**

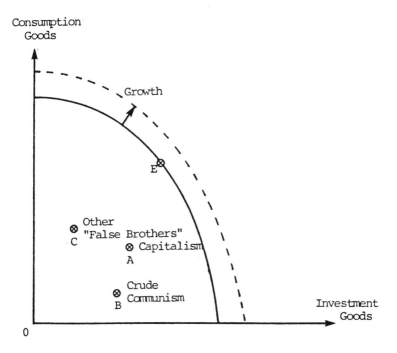

These points depict the underutilization of given resources at a given point in time. The conditions of alienated and "forced" labor exist in all of these systems. Under all these institutional frameworks, man is always "fragmented"; the ideal of a "total" man cannot be attained. Any point of the "production possibilities curve," such as point E, represents the realm of freedom. There will be no more "forced labor," no more alienation, and the condition of full development of both society and man will be fulfilled. Socialist humanism will prevail.

The Romantic movement also left a strong imprint on John Stuart Mill's restatement of classical political economy. It is well known that Mill's father James spared no effort in educating his son in accordance with the spirit of the Enlightenment (proper education would produce the perfectly rational person). Under his father's stern tutelage, Mill began to learn Greek at the tender age of three; by the age of eight he had begun to learn Latin; by twelve he went on to study literature, philosophy, history, government, and mathematics. At thirteen he began to study Ricardian economics, for his father was a staunch supporter of Ricardo. Unfortunately in 1826, John Stuart Mill, the perfect specimen of the Age of Enlightenment, experienced a mental crisis: he began to explore the writings of such English romanticists as Thomas Carlyle (1795–1881), William Wordsworth (1770–1850), and Samuel Taylor Coleridge (1772–1834). He was also exposed to the ideas of the "utopian socialists" (such as Saint-Simon, Owen, and Fourier). In 1830 Mill met Mrs. Harriet Taylor (1807–58) and, in the same year, he was introduced to the Saint-Simonians. It was Harriet Taylor who influenced Mill's views about the rights of women, humanitarianism, and liberty.[24] The utopian socialists opened his eyes to the importance of social justice and the undesirable aspects of industrial growth. The following passage from Mill on the question of the "stationary state" has been highly praised by modern antigrowth theorists.

> It must always have been seen, more or less distinctly, by political economists, that the increase in wealth is not boundless: that at the end of what they term the progressive state lies the stationary state, that all progress in wealth is but a postponement of this, and that each step in advance is an approach to it. . . . I cannot . . . regard the stationary state of capital and wealth with the unaffected aversion so generally manifested towards it *by political economists of the old school* [such as Ricardo]. *I am inclined to believe that it would be, on the whole, a very considerable improvement on our present condition.* I confess I am not charmed with the ideal of life held out by those who think that the normal state of human beings is that of struggling to get on; that the trampling, crushing, elbowing, and treading on each other's heels which comes from the existing type of social life, are the most desirable lot of human kind, or anything but the disagreeable symptoms of one of the phases of industrial progress. . . . It is scarcely necessary to remark that a *stationary condition of capital and population implies no stationary state of human improvement.* There would be as much scope as ever for all kinds of

mental culture, and moral and social progress; as much for improving the Art of Living and much more likelihood of its being improved, when minds cease to be engrossed by the art of getting on.[25]

Mill's *Principles of Political Economy with Some of Their Applications to Social Philosophy* and Marx and Engels's *Manifesto of the Communist Party* were published in the same fateful year—1844. "Karl Marx and John Stuart Mill were both strong critics of mid-nineteenth century industrial society," Graeme Duncan observes, "But their concerns, their range and their large background assumptions and presuppositions—and hence their critiques and their prescriptions—differ substantially. They were contemporaries who, despite their significance as the theorists and organizers of very different schools and movements paid little attention to each other."[26] The Romantic movement influenced their views in different ways. Marx was the revolutionary, whereas Mill was the gradualist who believed in evolutionary institutional changes within the system.

Notes

1. Bruce Wilshire, ed., *Romanticism and Evolution: The Nineteenth Century* (New York: Capricorn Books, 1968), p. 9.
2. T.Z. Lavine, *From Socrates to Sartre: The Philosophic Quest* (New York: Bantam Books, 1984), p. 203.
3. Ibid., pp. 196–97.
4. Ibid., p. 204.
5. Bruce Wilshire, *Romanticism and Evolution*, p. 16.
6. H.G. Schenk, *The Mind of the European Romantics* (Garden City, NY: Doubleday, 1969), pp. 23–24.
7. T.Z. Lavine, *From Socrates to Sartre*, p. 217.
8. Ibid.
9. José Ortega y Gasset, *The Revolt of the Masses* (New York: W.W. Norton, 1932).
10. Leszek Kolakowski, *The Alienation of Reason: A History of Positivist Thought* (Garden City, NY: Doubleday, 1969), p. 45.
11. Ibid., p. 51.
12. Murray N. Rothbard, "The Mantel of Science," in Helmut Schoek and James W. Wiggins, ed., *Scientism and Values* (Princeton, NJ: D. Van Nostrand, 1960), p. 159.

13. See Paul Davies, *The Cosmic Blueprint* (New York: Simon & Schuster, 1988), pp. 107–108.

14. Ibid., p. 98.

15. Joseph A. Schumpeter, *History of Economic Analysis*, p. 421.

16. Ibid., pp. 422–23.

17. See Homa Katouzian, *Ideology and Method in Economics* (New York: New York University Press, 1980), p. 36.

18. Ben B. Seligman, *Main Currents in Modern Economics: Economic Thought since 1870* (Glencoe, IL: The Free Press, 1962), p. 393. Ben B. Seligman pointed out the quotation was first cited by Theo Suranyi-Unger in *Economics in the Twentieth Century* (New York: 1931), p. 128.

19. Karl Marx and Friedrich Engels, *Manifesto of the Communist Party*, in Marx and Engels, *Basic Writings on Politics and Philosophy*, ed. by Lewis S. Feuer (Garden City, NY: Anchor Books, Doubleday, 1959), p. 32.

20. Schumpeter, *History of Economic Analysis*, p. 494.

21. Ibid., p. 496.

22. Michael Bleaney, *Underconsumption Theories: A History and Critical Analysis* (New York: International Publishers, 1976), p. 70.

23. Ivan Svitak, "The Sources of Socialist Humanism," in *Socialist Humanism: An International Symposium*, ed. by Eric Fromm (Garden City, NY: Anchor Books, Doubleday, 1966), pp. 20–21. Emphasis added.

24. Mill attributed to Harriet Taylor his humanitarianism, his hope and faith in human progress, his love of liberty, and his passionate defense of the rights of women. Mill called his writings both before and after their marriage the joint product of their minds. Among his works, Mill claimed that the following were their joint products: "Enfranchisement of Women" (1851), "On Liberty" (1859), "Considerations of Representative Government" (1861), and "Subjection of Women" (1869).

25. John Stuart Mill, *Principles of Political Economy with Some of Their Applications to Social Philosophy* (London: John W. Parker and Son, 1957), vol. 2, pp. 320–26. Emphasis added.

26. Graeme Duncan, *Marx and Mill* (Cambridge: Cambridge University Press, 1973), p. 1.

Chapter 3

Thermodynamics and the Newtonian World View

Newtonian time is symmetrical: the arrow of time can point either way; there is no distinction between "time forwards" and "time backwards." Darwinian theory of evolution involved a distinct progression or "arrow of time." However, Nicholas Georgescu-Roegen observes:

> It is physics again that supplies the only clear example of an evolutionary law: the Second Law of Thermodynamics, called also the Entropy Law.[1]

The purpose of this chapter is to consider the impact of the entropy law on the Newtonian mechanical world view and on orthodox economics modeled after Newtonian physics.

The Second Law of Thermodynamics

Newtonian mechanics did not cover the study of heat and other forms of energy and the various related changes in physical quantities such as temperature, pressure, or density. The study of such complicated mechanical systems is the subject of thermodynamics.

The second law was first formulated by the French engineer Sadi Carnot in 1824 in his study of the efficiency of steam engines. Carnot recorded his findings in his memoir, highlighting the fact that heat always moves by itself from hotter to colder bodies. As Georgescu-Roegen points out, laws of mechanics cannot account for a unidirectional movement. Hence a new branch of physics using nonmechanical explanations had to be created and thermodynamics was born.[2] By 1865, Rudolf Julius Clausius gave the classic formulation of the two laws of thermodynamics. The first law states that the energy of the universe remains constant; the second law states that the entropy of the universe at all times moves toward a maximum. The early prognosis of the entropy arrow of time was very gloomy. The universe is doomed, claimed the German physicist Hermann von Helmholtz in 1854. Why? Because the universe keeps on depleting its stock of available, potent energy, dissipating it into useless waste heat. The universe is slowly dying, choking in its own entropy. This impending doom was referred to as "the heat death."

The nonmechanical nature of thermodynamics was at first very difficult for physicists and other scientists to accept. Georgescu-Roegen points out that:

> Because the only way man can act upon matter directly is by pushing and pulling, we cannot easily conceive any agent in the physical universe that would have a different power. As Lord Kelvin, especially, emphasized, the human mind can comprehend a phenomenon clearly only if it can represent that phenomenon by a mechanical model. No wonder then that *ever since thermodynamics appeared on the scene, physicists bent their efforts to reduce heat phenomenon to locomotion*. The result is a new thermodynamics, better known by the name of *statistical mechanics*.[3]

Following Alvin Toffler,[4] the main focus of physics in the second half of the nineteenth century shifted from Newtonian dynamics to thermodynamics. It will be recalled that in Newtonian dynamics, "time" is reversible. However, according to the second law of thermodynamics, the universe cannot run backward to make up for entropy. Events cannot replay themselves. And this is what Sir Arthur Eddington called "time's arrow."[5] The different concepts of time created a deep crisis in both science and philosophy. Prigogine and Stengers call the crisis in science "the clash of doctrines" between thermodynamics and classical dynamics.[6] The entropy law also conflicts with Darwinian theory of evolution. As mentioned in chapter 2, Darwinian evolution implies that the universe, as time goes by, gets better organized and advances to higher forms of life. Hence, Darwinian theory points in the exact opposite direction of the second law of thermodynamics.

The clash of doctrines between biology and physics was partially solved by Ludwig Boltzmann's statistical interpretation of the second law of thermodynamics. Following James Clerk Maxwell's footsteps, Boltzmann introduced probability in physics as an explanatory principle. According to Prigogine and Stengers, Boltzmann was a great admirer of Darwin. His ambition was to become the "Darwin" of the evolution of matter. In applying probability theory, Boltzmann approached the question of entropy not at the level of individual trajectories as envisioned in Newtonian dynamics, but at the level of a population of molecules. "This, Boltzmann felt, was virtually tantamount to accomplishing Darwin's feat, but this time in physics: the driving force behind biological evolution—natural selection—cannot be defined for one individual but only for a large population. It is therefore a statistical concept."[7]

In the view of Prigogine and Stengers, Boltzmann's breakthrough accomplished two things: (a) a principle of molecular evolution had been produced—in other words, Boltzmann had opened the door to the microscopic interpretation of entropy; and (b) Boltzmann had taken a decisive step in the direction of the "physics of processes." "What determines temporal evolution in Boltzmann's equation is no longer the Hamiltonian, depending on the type of forces; now on the contrary, functions associated with the processes will generate motion."[8]

There was another question related to the entropy law, namely,

"To what extent are conscious beings subject to the second law?" Arthur Eddington observed: "The way in which conscious purpose might intervene was pointed out by Clerk Maxwell who invented a famous 'sorting demon.' "[9]

"Maxwell's demon" compels us to recognize the categorical differences between "shuffling" and "sorting." The "shuffling" in the universe goes on by itself. It is automatic. "Sorting," as Eddington puts it, "is the prerogative of mind or instinct."[10] Man's economic activity is similar to the sorting of "Maxwell's demon" —sorting for free energy (low entropy). A subjective element was thus introduced to the laws of thermodynamics. According to Eddington, "Thus effectively the demon reverses the signpost of time. Being a sorting agent, he is the embodiment of anti-chance."[11] Maybe there is justification for economists to talk about the circular flow of economic activity.

Thermodynamics and Economics

"A curious event in the history of economic thought," writes Georgescu-Roegen, "is that, years after the mechanistic dogma has lost its supremacy in physics and its grip on the philosophical world, the founders of [the] neoclassical school set out to erect an economic science after the pattern of mechanics—in the words of Jevons, as 'the mechanics of utility and self-interest.' "[12] The only outstanding exception, perhaps, is Alfred Marshall, who recognized the first law of thermodynamics:

> Man cannot create material things. In the mental and moral world indeed he may produce new ideas; but when he is said to produce material things, he really only produces utilities; or in other words, his efforts and sacrifices result in changing the form or arrangement of matter to adapt it better for the satisfaction of wants.[13]

The last sentence of this famous passage suggests that Marshall probably was acquainted with the statistical entropy law. However, he did not make any explicit statement on the matter.

Marshall also recognized the interrelationship between biology and economics. In 1920, he made this intuitive statement: "The Mecca of the economist lies in economic biology rather than economic dynamics."[14] Had he pursued this line of thought further, Marshall might have come close to the concept of the "optimistic arrow of time."

Economic scarcity is a reflection of the laws of thermodynamics. The fundamental nonmechanistic nature of the economic process is revealed by the entropy law. The economic process is, in a sense, like Maxwell's demon, sorting for free energy. During the "great growth controversies" of the late 1960s and early 1970s, a political economy of finite wants and nongrowth emerged. Herman E. Daly observes that "Arguments stressing ecologically sound limits to wealth and population have been made by Boulding and by Spengler (both past presidents of the American Economic Association). [Subsequently] E.J. Mishan, Tibor Scitovsky, and Staffan Linder have made penetrating antigrowth arguments."[15]

A new political economy requires new concepts and a new vocabulary; these have been defined and formulated by Daly,[16] who put the Fisherian theory of capital and interest in juxtaposition with the new visions and analyses of Boulding and Georgescu-Roegen for the formulation of the new concepts and vocabularies of antigrowth arguments. The Fisherian concepts of capital and interest may be stated symbolically as $W = Y/r$, where capital or wealth is represented by W; the flow of income derived from capital is designated by Y; and the rate of interest is represented by r. The equation may be stated alternatively as $rW = Y$. Capital, of course, is a stock variable that will wear out and must be replaced. This continual maintenance and replacement activity is an unavoidable cost. Daly calls this process "a continual throughput of matter-energy" (the term "throughput" is part of the new vocabulary).

In "The Economics of the Coming Spaceship Earth" Boulding distinguishes between "open economy" (before the recognition of the "pessimistic time's arrow"), which he picturesquely calls the "cowboy economy," and the "closed economy" of the future, for which he coins the term "spaceman economy" (this is similar to Georgescu-Roegen's "unidirectional irrevocable evolution"). According to Boulding, the difference between the "cowboy economy" and the "spaceman economy" is most apparent in the attitude of consumption. In the former, consumption is regarded as a good thing, and is production. In the "spaceman economy," on the other hand, the essential measure of the success of the economy is not production and consumption at all, but the nature, extent, quality, and complexity of the total capital stock.[17]

The majority of antigrowth theorists argue that since exponential growth in a finite world leads to disaster of all kinds, ecological salvation lies in the stationary state (or steady state) in the sense expressed by John Stuart Mill:

> It is scarcely necessary to remark that a stationary condition of capital and population implies no stationary state of human improvement. There would be as much scope as ever for all kinds of mental culture, a moral and social progress.[18]

In the 1970s, there was an explosion of antigrowth literature. It is beyond the scope of this book to cover all the relevant arguments but we hope that the passages quoted in this section convey some of the flavor of these theories.

Thermodynamics and Philosophy

The link between physics (thermodynamics) and economics (antigrowth theories) has been briefly considered in the preceding sections. The philosophy underlying the antigrowth theories merits more explicit consideration. One can detect in the ethical assumptions of contemporary antigrowth theorists a mixture of the traditions of Christianity and oriental religious teachings with a sprinkling of classical Greek philosophy.[19] In general, these theorists embrace the organic view of nature and reject the Newtonian mechanics. Their approach is holistic and antireductionistic. In one way or another, they all reject growthmania and money fetishism and prefer some feasible "small is beautiful" plan to postpone the doomsday. For example: The holistic approach of E.F. Schumacher is clearly conveyed in his emphasis on the concept of "meta-economics," which consists of two parts: one dealing with man and the other dealing with the environment. According to Schumacher, the market represents only the surface of society. Its significance relates to the monetary situation as it exists there and then. "In a sense," he stresses, "the market is the institutionalization of individualism and non-responsibility. Neither buyer nor seller is responsible for anything but himself."[20]

In the study of meta-economics, Schumacher accepts the traditions of Christianity, Buddhism, and Ghandi. He asserts that the following ethical clues should be emphasized: (a) smallness, (b) simplicity, (c) capital saving, and (d) nonviolence.

The steady-state economy position of Daly is arrived at by deductions from the following first principles: (a) enoughness, (b) stewardship, (c) humility, and (d) holism.[21] Daly's first principles are in the context of the Christian tradition.

The tradition of Christianity is also followed by E.J. Mishan, who takes issue with the growth of "permissiveness" in modern society. Mishan emphasizes that man has been all too successful in his search for mastery over nature. His appetite has fed on his success. "Today there are no bounds to his ambition, and no limits to his capacity. He has begun to wreck the social order as surely as he has begun to wreck the natural order."[22]

The impact of thermodynamics on philosophy is much deeper than the philosophical underpinnings of modern antigrowth theories mentioned above. The introduction of the irreversible arrow of time by the second law of thermodynamics created two important clashes of doctrines in the nineteenth century, namely: (a) the deep rift between philosophy and Newtonian physics, and (b) the controversies between Newtonian dynamics and thermodynamics.

The introduction of the "irreversible time" by the entropy law was part of the spirit of time in the nineteenth century. As we have said, the nineteenth century was a century during which the process of "becoming" and evolution was prominent. It was a century in which biology overshadowed Newtonian physics. The global intellectual movement was reflected in the "Romantic Revolt" against the narrow dogmatism of the Enlightenment. The history of modern philosophy may be considered as a continuous warfare of physics and the philosophy of evolution.

It will be recalled that the basic processes of nature were considered by classical physicists to be deterministic and time-symmetrical (reversible time). Newtonian mechanics emphasized the universality and eternal character of natural laws, independent of time. In the words of Stephen W. Hawking, "The Laws of science do not distinguish between the past and the future."[23] In this sense, Newtonian physics is similar to the Aristotelian concept of a divine and immutable heaven. Prigogine and Stengers write: "In Aristotle's opinion, it was only the heavenly world to which we could hope to apply an exact mathematical description."[24] Whereas on earth, Aristotle believed in teleology (becoming) and natural diversity. Both "becoming" and "diversity" were ruled out by Newtonian physics for the sake of universality. "In this sense," say Prigogine and Stengers, "classical science brought heaven [Aristotelian] to earth. However, this apparently was not the intention of the fathers of modern science."[25]

In the twentieth century, the deep rift between philosophy and physics was brought to the surface by the clash between the philosopher Henri Bergson (1859–1941) and Albert Einstein that took place at the Société de Philosophie in Paris on April 6, 1922. Bergson was critical of the mechanistic world view and the abolishing of the process of "becoming" in Newtonian physics. He argued that time is as fundamental as space and that time holds the essence of life. Because time is an accumulation that arises at every step of human experience, the future cannot be the same as the past. In *Creative Evolution* (1907), Bergson emphasized that geometrical predictability of all things, which is the goal of a mechanistic science, is only an intellectual delusion. He pointed out that memory is the handmaiden of time and that for an individual, existence means creative evolution. As John D. Barrow and Frank J. Tipler observe:

> [Bergson's] philosophy is based on "Becoming," or the temporal aspects of reality, as the fundamental metaphysical concept. "Being," or existence, is the basic metaphysics entity in the Cartesian philosophical tradition which was the dominant influence in French philosophical tradition before Bergson. In philosophies of Being time or more generally evolution, is regarded as illusory or of no fundamental importance.[26]

Einstein, on the other hand, according to Prigogine and Stengers, "appears as the incarnation of the drive toward a formulation of physics in which no reference to irreversibility would be made on the fundamental level."[27] Thus, at the Paris Société de Philosophie, Einstein rejected Bergson's view. "For him distinctions among past, present, and future were outside the scope of physics."[28]

As far as the rift between classical dynamics and thermodynamics is concerned, we may recall that all the properties of classical dynamics can be summarized in terms of a single function, the Hamiltonian (see chapter 1), the canonical equations of which, as we have seen, are reversible. For example, in the Optimal neoclassical growth model stated in chapter 1, the Hamiltonian function is written as:

$$H(c,k,\mu) = u(c) + \dot{\mu}k = U[f(k) - nk - \dot{k}] + \mu [f(k) - nk - c].$$

The two canonical equations derived from the Hamiltonian function are:

$$\delta H/\delta k = - \dot{\mu}, \text{ and } \delta H/\delta \mu = \dot{k}.$$

They contain the general properties of all dynamic change in the given optimal growth model. As Prigogine and Stengers point out, "The canonical equations are reversible: time inversion is mathematically the equivalent of velocity inversion."[29] Let us borrow an illustration of "reversible time" from Stephen W. Hawking to illustrate the point: suppose a cup of water is falling off a table and breaking into pieces on the floor. If one takes a film of this event and runs the film backward, one will see that the pieces suddenly gather themselves together off the floor and jump back to form a whole cup on the table.[30] Hawking writes: "The reason that in real life we don't see this reversible phenomenon is that it is forbidden by the second law of thermodynamics."[31]

Fortunately, after the second revolution in physics and the advance of the theory of chaos, a new synthesis is emerging and all the deep rifts and controversies are beginning to be resolved. These new developments are considered in the next three chapters on relativity theory, quantum mechanics, and chaos.

Notes

1. Nicholas Georgescu-Roegen, *The Entropy Law and the Economic Process* (Cambridge, MA: Harvard University Press, 1971), pp. 128–29.
2. See ibid., p. 129.
3. Ibid., p. 141. Emphasis added.
4. See Alvin Toffler, "Foreword," in *Order out of Chaos* by Ilya Prigogine and Isabelle Stengers, (New York: Bantam, 1984).
5. Sir Arthur Eddington, *The Nature of the Physical World* (Ann Arbor: University of Michigan Press, 1958), p. 68.
6. Prigogine and Stengers, *Order out of Chaos*, chap. 8.
7. See ibid., p. 240–41.
8. Ibid., p. 242–43.
9. Sir Arthur Eddington, *New Pathways in Science* (Ann Arbor: University of Michigan Press, 1959), p. 68. Eddington described the "sorting demon" as follows:

> the adjacent vessels contain gas at the same uniform temperature; between them there is a very small door. At the door there stands a demon. Whenever he sees in the left-hand vessel an unusually fast-moving molecule approaching the door, he opens it so that the molecule goes through into the right-hand vessel; for slow-moving molecules he keeps the door shut and they rebound into the left-hand vessel. Similarly, he allows the slow-moving molecules from the right-hand vessel to pass through the left. The result is that he concentrates fast motion in the right-hand vessel and slow-motion in the left-hand vessel; or since the speed of the molecule motion corresponds to temperature, the right-hand vessel becomes hot and the left-hand vessel cool. Maxwell's demon overrides the second law of thermodynamics. [pp. 68–69]

10. Eddington, *The Nature of the Physical World*, p. 93.

11. Eddington, *New Pathways*, p. 68.

12. Georgescu-Roegen, "The Entropy Law and The Economic Problem," reprinted in Herman E. Daly ed., *Economics, Ecology, Ethics* (San Francisco: W.H. Freeman, 1980), p. 49.

13. Alfred Marshall, *Principles of Economics,* 8th ed. (New York: Macmillan, 1920), p. 63.

14. Ibid., p. xiv.

15. Herman E. Daly, ed., *Toward a Steady-State Economy* (San Francisco: W.H. Freeman, 1973), p. 24. A supplementary short list of antigrowth theorists is as follows: E.F. Schumacher ("Small is Beautiful"), Nicholas Georgescu-Roegen ("The Entropy Law and the Economic Process"), Donella H. Meadows, Dennis L. Meadows, et al. ("The Limits of Growth"), Paul R. and Anne H. Ehrich, Garret Hardin, Earl Cook, John Cobb, E.J. Mishan, and Jeremy Rifkin ("Entropy: A New World View"). The writings of some of these authors are reprinted in Daly, *Toward a Steady-State Economy* and in *Economics, Ecology, Ethics.*

16. Daly, "The Concept of Steady-State Economy," in *Toward a Steady-State Economy*, p. 24.

17. See Kenneth E. Boulding, "The Economics of the Coming Spaceship Earth," in Daly, *Toward a Steady-State Economy*, p. 127.

18. John Stuart Mill, *Principles of Political Economy* (London: John W. Parker and Son, 1857), vol. 2, p. 326.

19. See E.F. Schumacher, "The Age of Plenty: A Christian View" (1974) in Daly, *Economics, Ecology, Ethics,* pp. 127–37; E.F. Schumacher, "Buddhist Economics," *Resurgence 1*, 11 (January–February 1968), also in Daly, *Economics, Ecology, Ethics*, pp. 138–45; and E.J. Mishan, "The Growth of Affluence and the Decline of Welfare," in Daly, *Economics, Ecology, Ethics*, pp. 267–81.

20. E.F. Schumacher, *Small is Beautiful: Economics as if People Mattered* (New York: Harper & Row, 1973), pp. 44–51.

21. Herman E. Daly, *Steady-State Economics*, p. 46.

22. E.J. Mishan, "The Growth of Affluence and the Decline of Welfare," in Daly, ed., *Economics, Ecology, Ethics*, p. 276.

23. Stephen W. Hawking, *A Brief History of Time* (New York: Bantam, 1988), p. 144.

24. Prigogine and Stengers, *Order out of Chaos*, p. 305.

25. Ibid.

26. John D. Barrow and Frank J. Tipler, *The Anthropic Cosmological Principle* (New York: Oxford University Press, 1986), p. 189.

27. Prigogine and Stengers, *Order out of Chaos*, p. 294.

28. Ibid.

29. Ibid., p. 71.

30. See Stephen W. Hawking, *A Brief History of Time*, p. 144.

31. Ibid.

Chapter 4

Relativity, Philosophy, and Economics

The second revolution in physics consists of two earth-shaking theories: (a) Albert Einstein's theory of relativity, and (b) quantum mechanics. The former redefines the outer limits of man's knowledge, such as the concepts of space, time, gravitation, and motion; the latter penetrates deeper into the problems concerning the basic units of matter and energy. This chapter considers some important implications of relativity theory for philosophy and economics. Quantum mechanics and its shock waves are the subject of chapter 5.

The absolute concepts in Newtonian physics were space, time, length, mass, and infinite velocity, or infinite speed of transmission of signals or information. With regard to the first two absolute concepts, Newton wrote: "Absolute space, in its own nature, without relation to anything external, remains always similar and immovable." "Absolute, true, and mathematical time, of itself, and from its own nature, flows equably without relation to anything external."[1] These suppositions of Newton, in conjunction with the adoption of a Euclidean reference frame that extends through all space and endures for all time, justify the existence of one ideal overall frame of reference for motion of the absolute masses. With all the absolute concepts everything would fall neatly into place. Absolute simultaneity between two distant events regardless of the motion of the observer follows naturally from the assumptions of absolute time and infinite velocity. The assumption of absolute space provided one homogenous global inertial frame of reference. In the words of Prigogine and Stengers, "This is the reason for [Newtonian physics'] claim to universality, why it can be applied in the same way whatever the scale of the objects: the motion of atoms, planets, and stars are governed by a single law."[2] Thus, Newtonian physics' conquest of the intellectual world was more complete than Ricardo's conquest of England.[3]

The assumptions of absolute time and invariant velocity were behind the rationale of the Galilean transformation and the common-sense law that the relative velocity of two moving bodies is the sum of the two individual velocities. What is the Galilean transformation? In the first place, the principle of relativity states that all laws of physics are the same in every inertial frame of reference. (The term "inertial" means that all isolated bodies move in a straight line with constant velocity; frame of reference refers to a "coordinate system." The "inertial frame" is sometimes called the "Galilean frame" in honor of Galileo.) We turn now to the question of the Galilean transformation; in the simplest sense, it has to do with the principle of relativity. The Galilean transformation is a system of mathematical equations relating the three space coordinates (x, y, z) and one time coordinate (t) observed on the first Galilean frame, which is relatively at rest, with the four coordinates (x', y', z', t') of the second Galilean frame, which is moving. With a view to determining the invariant law of physics involved in this situation, the Galilean transformation laws are invoked. The mathematical equations involved may be stated as follows:

$$x = x' + vt'; t = t', \text{ and}$$
$$x' = x + vt; t' = t$$

where x and x' denote the positions of bodies in the two Galilean frames; v signifies the invariant velocity; and the two equations: $t = t'$ and $t' = t$ indicate absolute time. The Galilean transformation states that the substitution of the second coordinates (x', y', z') for the coordinates (x, y, z) of the first reference frame would not change the form of the equations. Thus, the invariants of the transformation are the aforementioned equations. They are the law of physics involved in this particular case; thus, they are the same in every inertial frame of reference (which is the principle of relativity).

It is clear that the principle of relativity does not mean that everything in the universe is relative. Bertrand Russell points out that, "This is, of course, because, if everything was relative, there would be nothing for it to be relative to."[4] One should also keep in mind that Einstein's theory of relativity has the same objective as the Galilean-Newtonian principle of relativity. This assertion may be supported by the first fundamental principle of Einstein's Special Theory of Relativity (1905) which states that all inertial frames are equivalent with respect to all laws of physics. Einstein's theory could be considered as an extension or generalization of the classical principle to all classes of phenomena. Hence A. d'Abro suggests that "the theory of relativity might also be termed the 'quest of the absolute.' "[5] In the same vein, Nigel Calder comments to the effect that Einstein's relativity theory could be called "invariance theory."[6] Einstein's quest of the absolute has been most perceptively illustrated by Bertrand Russell as follows:

> If you know that one man is twice as rich as another, this fact must appear equally whether you estimate the wealth of both in pounds or dollars or francs or any other currency. The numbers representing their fortunes will be changed, but one number will always be double the other.[7]

Relativity simply means that the invariant truth (one man is twice as rich as another) can be expressed in various ways (in pounds or dollars or any other currency). All relativities of Einstein's theory are of this type.

Before we consider Einstein's generalization of the classical principle, we are reminded of an earlier irony in history. It will be recalled that the Renaissance scientists, such as Copernicus, Kepler, Galileo, and Newton, were devoted followers of the Christian faith. They sought in their research a better understanding of God's blueprint of nature. It was not their original intention to produce physical laws that would ultimately clash with Church doctrines. It is similarly ironic that Einstein's generalization of Newtonian physics should ultimately undermine the domination of the mechanistic world view for the past three centuries.

Einstein's Special Theory of Relativity (1905)

Einstein called his 1905 theory the "special theory" because he confined his analysis of relative velocity between different inertial reference frames. Thus, Einstein realized that he had not pushed the "quest of the absolute" far enough and that he had not considered gravitational phenomena. In his special theory Einstein was mainly concerned with electromagnetic phenomena (light is an electromagnetic phenomenon), as evidenced by his second fundamental principle of the special theory: the speed of light in empty space always has the same value. The constant velocity of light is denoted by the letter c ($c = 300,000$ km/sec). This fundamental principle has been fully justified by experiment.[8]

The constant velocity of light, c, is the first new universal constant introduced into the Newtonian physics. It is the limiting velocity for the propagation of all signals. Hence, it modified the Newtonian assumption of infinite speed of propagation and limited the region in space for any individual observer. In other words, the introduction of the new universal constant creates nonhomogeneous physical scales in a Newtonian homogeneous universe. One can no longer define the absolute simultaneity of two distant events. Simultaneity is relative for it can only be defined in terms of a given reference frame. An analog of this limit is the budget constraint of an individual consumer in microeconomics. It defines the consumption frontier that the individual cannot transgress.

The connection between the constant velocity of light and relative simultaneity is demonstrated by the following equation:

$$\text{Relative velocity} = (v_1 + v_2)/(1 + v_1v_2/c^2)$$

where the v_1 and v_2 stand for two moving inertial reference frames; c denotes the constant speed of light. The denominator $(1 + v_1v_2/c^2)$ is often referred to as the relativistic factor. The Einsteinian relative-velocity equation is different from the classical equation for relative velocity. As mentioned earlier, classical relative velocity = $v_1 + v_2$. Once the new universal constant (c = 300,000 km/sec) is introduced, the classical equation runs into trouble. To illustrate this point, we borrow a numerical example from Eric Chaison[9]: Suppose two rocket ships move toward one another, one at a velocity of 150,000 km/sec, the other at 200,000 km/sec. Each ship is traveling below the velocity of light. However, the sum of their velocities would be 350,000 km/sec which exceeds the limit imposed by c.

The introduction of the new universal constant not only destroys Newtonian physics' claim to universality, but also demolishes the Cartesian-Newtonian assumption that the observer observes but does not disturb nature. In the words of Prigogine and Stengers, "The fact that relativity is based on a constraint that applies only to physically localized observers, to beings who can be in only one place at a time and not everywhere at once, gives this physics a 'human' quality. . . . It is a physics that presupposes an observer situated within the observed world."[10] In other words, it changes man's dialog with nature.

Since every reference system (or coordinate system) has its own particular time, there is no such thing as a space interval independent of time. Thus, Einstein's special theory also revolutionized our concepts of space and time. We must accept that time is not independent of space, but is combined with it to form a four-dimensional space-time. The fundamental concept in relativity theory is an event, which is specified not only by space but also by a time of happening.

To recapitulate, Einstein's new universal constant has displaced four absolute concepts of classical physics: absolute space, absolute time, invariant speed of propagation, and absolute simultaneity. In addition, it has put an end to the claim to universality of Newtonian physics.

Relativity, however, does not mean abandonment of the quest for absolute laws of physics. In Bertrand Russell's words:

> physics is intended to give information about what really occurs in the physical world, and not only about the private perceptions of separate observers. Physics must, therefore, be concerned with those features which a physical process has in common for all observers since such features alone can be regarded as belonging to the physical occurrence itself.[11]

In accomplishing this central task, Einstein found ready to his hand the mathematical instrument called the Lorentz transformation, which according to Russell, "embodies the whole mathematical essence of the special theory of relativity."[12] By using the mathematical equations of the "Einstein-Lorentz transformation," Einstein was able to attain the double objective: (a) to find the common relation, or the "residue" independent of the different observers, and (b) to preserve the second fundamental principle of his special theory.

What is the "Einstein-Lorentz transformation"? It is a system of equations relating distance denoted by the symbol x' and time represented by the letter t' observed on a moving reference frame A (suppose this reference frame is a moving train with a constant speed or velocity signified by v') with the distance, x, and time, t, observed on reference frame B (suppose it is the embankment). Einstein raised the question:

> Can we conceive of a relation between place and time of the individual events relative to both reference-bodies, such that every ray of

light possesses the velocity of transmission c relative to the embankment and relative to the train? This question leads to a quite definite positive answer, and to a perfectly definite transformation law for space-time magnitudes of an event when changing over from one body of reference to another.[13]

This problem is solved by the following equations:

(1) $$x' = (x - vt)/\sqrt{(1 - v^2/c^2)}$$

(2) $$y' = y$$

(3) $$z' = z$$

(4) $$t' = (t - vx/c^2)/\sqrt{(1 - v^2/c^2)}.$$

This system of equations is known as the Einstein-Lorentz transformation. A light signal is sent and advances in accordance with the equation:

(5) $$x = ct.$$

If we substitute for x the value ct in equations (1) and (4) of the Einstein-Lorentz transformation, we obtain the following equations:

(6) $$x' = (c - v)t/\sqrt{(1 - v^2/c^2)}$$

(7) $$t' = (1 - v/c)t/\sqrt{(1 - v^2/c^2)}.$$

From which, by division, follows immediately this expression[14]:

(8) $$x' = ct'.$$

It should be noted that equations (5) $x = ct$ and (8) $x' = ct'$ represent the invariants in space-time and that both distance x' and time t' of equations (1) and (4) are dependent on the Lorentz contraction factor represented by the expression $(1 - v^2/c^2)$.

In fact, the same factor enters into every other measurement in space-time. The following are examples:

(1) *Slowing down of a moving clock*: (Time between ticks of a moving clock)/(Time between ticks of a stationary clock) = $1/\sqrt{(1 - v^2/c^2)}$.

(2) *Contraction of the length of a moving body*: "An object moving with a velocity v, relating to the observer is contracted in the ratio $\sqrt{(1 - v^2/c^2)}$ in a direction parallel to its motion as compared with an identical object at rest relative to the observer."[15]

(3) *Varying of mass with velocity*: $m = m_0/\sqrt{(1 - v^2/c^2)}$, where m stands for the mass of a body moving with velocity v; the numerator m_0 denotes the mass at rest.

(4) *Momentum and force*: $p = mv$, where p stands for the momentum of a body which is simply the product of its mass and its velocity. The definition is the same as that in Newtonian mechanics. It departs from the Newtonian definition. However, if one substitutes the new definition of mass as stated in (3), the Einsteinian definition is obtained:

$$p = m_0 v/\sqrt{(1 - v^2/c^2)}.$$

(5) *The equivalence of mass and energy*: Einstein's most famous equation, this destroyed the classical concept of absolute mass: $E = mc^2$. It states that the mass of a moving body increases as its motion increases. Since motion is kinetic energy, one can say that energy, E, has mass. If we substitute the new definition of mass as stated in (3) namely,

$$m = m_0/\sqrt{(1 - v^2/c^2)}$$

into $E = mc^2$, we will see the Lorentz factor lurking behind Einstein's most important equation:

$$E = mc^2 = m_0 c^2 / \sqrt{(1 - v^2/c^2)}.$$

With the examples stated above, we can now have a better understanding of Bertrand Russell's assertion that the equation of the Lorentz transformation embodies "the whole mathematical essence of the special theory of relativity." It is a valuable heuristic aid in Einstein's search for general laws of nature.

It should be noted that at the time of Einstein's revisions of classical physics in 1905, non-Euclidean geometry had been in existence for about seventy-five years. It will be recalled that non-Euclidean geometry was created by K.F. Gauss (1777–1855), N.I. Lobachevski (1793–1856), James Bolyai (1802–60), and B. Riemann (1826–66). One might say that this astonishing development in mathematics is another irony in intellectual history. What these audacious intellects had in mind when they undertook their research projects was to investigate the logical consequences of a new parallel axiom. It did not occur to them that their creation could, in the words of Morris Kline, rob "man of his most respected truths and perhaps even of the hope of ever attaining certainty about anything."[16]

In 1854 Bernard Riemann developed a non-Euclidean geometry using a generalized form of the calculus of vectors called "Tensor Calculus." In the view of Bertrand Russell:

> It is impossible without mathematics to explain the theory of the tensors; the non-mathematician must be content to know that it is the technical method by which we eliminate the conventional elements [*such as the Cartesian coordinates*] from our measurements and laws, and thus arrive at physical laws which are independent of the observer's point of view.[17]

In his "quest of the absolute," Einstein found ready to his hand the theory of the tensors.

The General Theory of Relativity (1915)

In the general theory, Einstein attempted to consider accelerating frames of reference and to incorporate gravitational phenomena. Stephen W. Hawking observes that "Einstein made a number of unsuccessful attempts between 1908 and 1914 to find a theory of gravity that was consistent with the special theory. Finally, in 1915 he proposed what we now call the general theory of relativity."[18]

Since all objective physical laws must be expressed mathematically by invariants and tensors in space-time, Einstein imposed the acid test or restriction with which all natural laws must comply. This was "the principle of the covariance of natural laws," or "the general principle of relativity." In 1915 Einstein found the covariance principle in the form of "the principle of equivalence of gravitation and inertia," which states in its simplest terms that there was no way to distinguish the motion produced by inertial forces (such as acceleration, recoil, centrifugal forces, etc.) from motion induced by gravitational forces. Hence Einstein made the revolutionary suggestion that one should stop thinking about the idea of "force of gravitation" altogether and use instead the language of non-Euclidean geometry in discussing gravitational effects.

With the aid of non-Euclidean geometry, Einstein suggested that space-time was not flat, as implied in his special theory. The four-dimensional space-time continuum is curved, or "warped," by the distribution of mass and energy within it. The motion of bodies like the earth is not due to attraction by the force of gravity. Rather their motion follows the nearest thing to a straight line in curved space-time, which is called a "geodesics" in Riemann geometry. "General relativity is therefore," according to Paul Davies, "an explanation of gravity as a distortion in the geometry of space-time."[19] And, according to John Archibald Wheeler, "Space tells matter how to move and matter tells space how to curve."[20]

If we are dealing with curved space-time, the classical Cartesian coordinate system must be replaced by a new order and

Figure 4.1. **Warped space-time continuum and gravitational field**

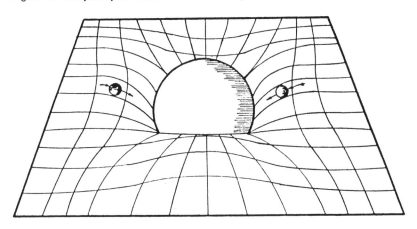

measurement. In Einstein's words, "the Gauss co-ordinate system has to take place in the body of reference. The following statement corresponds to the fundamental idea of the general principle of relativity: 'All Gaussian co-ordinate systems are essentially equivalent for the transformation of the general laws of nature.' "[21]

The curved space-time, as suggested by Einstein, creates "gravitational fields," which are analogous to Faraday's "magnetic fields." The "geodesics" of bodies are caused by the "gravitational fields," and not attracted by the force of gravity. This assertion is another manifestation of the covariance principle of natural laws. Figure 4.1 is a stylized depiction of the curved space-time continuum and the "gravitational fields."

Philosophical Consequences of Relativity Theory

F.S.C. Northrop observed that "any theory of physics makes more physical and philosophical assumptions than the facts alone give or imply. For this reason, any theory is subject to further modification and reconstruction with the advent of new evidence that is incompatible."[22] As pointed out by Northrop, Einstein's deduction "in his method runs not from facts to the assumptions of the theory but from the assumed theory to the facts and experimental data."[23]

Some of Einstein's assumptions are ontological. Ontology is that branch of philosophy that inquires about the reality status of a law or an entity. Einstein's incisive answer to the problem of objectivity and his "quest of the absolute" belong to ontology. In the view of Henry Margenau, Einstein's "criterion of objectivity lies somehow within the very structure of theory itself, that it must reside within some formal property of the ideal scheme which pretends to correspond to reality. And that is where the theory of relativity places it. Objectivity becomes equivalent to invariance of physical laws, not physical phenomena or observations."[24]

Some of Einstein's assumptions are epistemological. Epistemology is that branch of philosophy called the theory of knowledge. It asks questions such as: "How is our knowledge formulated, expressed, and communicated?" Einstein's revolutionary assertion that gravity is Riemann geometry and his introduction of the new universal constant, c, into classical physics are in the realm of epistemology.

What is the most important contribution of relativity theory? Werner Heisenberg, one of the founders of quantum mechanics (see chapter 5) answers this question as follows:

> The dissolution of the rigid frame of concepts of the nineteenth century took place in two distinct stages. The first was the discovery, through the theory of relativity, that even such fundamental concepts as space and time could be changed and in fact must be changed on account of new experience. . . . The second stage was the discussion of the concept of matter enforced by the experimental results concerning the atomic structure.[25]

One of the rigid concepts of the nineteenth century was absolute simultaneity, which was one of the foundation stones of the rigid relation between cause and effect, as well as the basic assumption of "free will" and determinism. Relativity theory upsets both of these time-honored beliefs. Once Einstein replaced the concept of absolute simultaneity with relative simultaneity, the rigid relation between cause and effect fell. In the words of Morris Kline,

> when we discussed the question of simultaneity we found that the order of the two flashes of light depended on the observer. If these two flashes were replaced by events that appeared to be cause and effect to some observers, there might, nevertheless, be other observers who could not view the events in that relation, for to them the event called the effect might occur before the cause. Revision of the concept is obviously in order.[26]

Relativity theory and the subsequent advance of quantum mechanics have forced modern philosophers to revise their approach to the thorny problem of free will and determinism. Sir James Jeans says: "Modern philosophy also seems to have come to the conclusion that there is no real alternative to determinism, with the result that the question now discussed is no longer whether we are free but why we think we are free."[27] To illustrate this point Jeans quotes Spinoza's remark "that a stone in the air would think itself free if it could forget the hand that had thrown it. . . . Thus free will is only our name for unconscious determinism."[28]

Another rigid concept destroyed by Einstein's new notions of structure is the concept of the absolute mass of the basic particle. According to David Bohm, "relativity implies that neither the point particles nor the quasi-rigid body can be taken as primary concepts. Rather, these have to be expressed in terms of events and processes."[29] The rejection of the mechanistic world view is also revealed by Einstein's continuous search for a unified field theory. "The classical idea of the separability of the world into distinct but interacting parts is no longer valid or relevant. Rather, we have to regard the universe as an undivided and unbroken whole."[30]

Did Einstein embrace the philosophy of idealism or that of empiricism? Although Einstein believed that "Being is always something which is mentally constructed by us,"[31] yet his philosophical position is quite different from the idealism of Kant. According to Hans Reichenbach, "Einstein has shown the way to a philosophy superior to the philosophy of the 'synthetic a priori.' It is the philosophy of empiricism into which Einstein's relativity belongs."[32] In the same vein as Henry Margenau, Reichenbach writes: "Einstein's empiricism is that of modern theoretical physics, the empiricism of mathematical construction which is so devised that it connects observational data by deductive operations and enables us to predict new observational data."[33] Thus, it is not the same as the empiricism of Francis Bacon and John Stuart Mill, who believed that all laws of nature could be found by simple inductive generalizations.

The dissolution of the rigid frame of concepts by the theory of relativity led to another paradoxical consequence. According to Bertrand Russell:

> physics tells much less about the physical world than we thought it did. . . . To the non-mathematical mind, the abstract character of our physical knowledge may seem unsatisfactory. From an artistic or imaginative point of view, it is perhaps regrettable, but from a practical point of view, it is of no consequence. . . . The final conclusion is that we know very little, and yet it is astonishing that we know so much, and still more astonishing that so little knowledge can give us so much power.[34]

(Just think of Einstein's most famous formula, $E = mc^2$, and atomic power.)

Relativity and Economics

Keynes was, probably, the first economist who recognized the importance of Einstein's theory of curved space-time. The following passage from his *General Theory of Employment, Interest and Money* provides us with strong evidence that Keynes was well acquainted with Einstein's general theory:

> The classical theorists resemble Euclidean geometers in a non-Euclidean world who, discovering that in experience straight lines

apparently parallel often meet, rebuke the lines for not keeping straight—as the only remedy for the unfortunate collisions which are occurring. Yet, in truth, there is no remedy except to throw over the axiom of parallels and to work out a non-Euclidean geometry. Something similar is required in economics. We need to throw over the second postulate of the classical doctrine and to work out the behavior of a system in which involuntary unemployment in the strict sense is possible.[35]

In light of the above quotation, it would not be an exaggeration to assert that Keynes's theory of involuntary unemployment was inspired by Einstein. It follows that the disequilibrium macroeconomics of Robert W. Clower and Axel Leijonhufvud as well as the economics of the "post-Keynesians"[36] are implicitly influenced by the theory of relativity.

Keynes may be considered one of the pioneers on the treatment of "irreversible time." According to Joan Robinson, "Keynes brought back time into economic theory. He woke the Sleeping Princess from the long oblivion to which 'equilibrium' and 'perfect foresight' had condemned her and let her out into the world here and now."[37] Did Einstein contribute anything to this development? The answer is probably negative. Hans Reichenbach observes: "The irreversibility of time does not find an expression in the theory of relativity."[38] Similarly, A. d'Abro writes: "To this mystery of the unidirectional passage of time, the theory of relativity contributes no new information, so that we may discuss the problem from the standpoint of classical science."[39] Hence, the emphasis on "historical time" of the general equilibrium theorists, "post-Keynesians," and the "new Austrian school" writers most likely is inspired by the law of entropy and the statistical reformulation of the law.

Einstein might have had an indirect influence on the methodology of economics through the tradition established by Karl Popper. The stranglehold of the logical positivists on economics has been well documented by economists. By invoking the principle of "Occam's razor," Hicks shaved off the philosophical element of utilitarianism from his "Hicksian revolution" and the exorcism performed by Samuelson in his revealed preference theory are two of the best-publicized illustrations of the influence of logical positivism. Although Popper was a personal friend of some members of the Vienna Circle, there are major doctrinal differences between Popper and the logical positivists. Popper holds that scientific theories are free creations of the mind, whereas logical positivists insist that primary hypotheses should be formed by direct sense-experience. Einstein's view is closer to that of Popper. In rejecting the "variability methodology" of the logical positivists, Popper introduced the new methodology of falsification. (Popper's falsification methodology is considered further in chapter 7.) Although Popper has not completely conquered the philosophy of science, he is certainly a force to be reckoned with in the area of economic methodology. Since Einstein's philosophy of science is closer to that of Popper, we therefore suggest that Einstein has had an indirect influence on economic methodology.

A more far-reaching influence of relativity theory on economics is revealed by the emerging holistic systems approach to economics. This is a natural consequence of the dissolution of the classical mechanistic world view. The credit of toppling of the mechanistic world view should be shared by Einstein, Niels Bohr, Heisenberg, and the exponents of the theory of chaos. The leading advocates of the systems approach to economic problems are Philip Mirowski, Fritjof Capra, Hazel Henderson, Ilya Prigogine and Isabelle Stengers, Eric Jantsch, Kenneth Boulding, and Benjamin Ward.[40]

Notes

1. Newton quoted in Edward F. Taylor and John Archibald Wheeler, *Space-Time Physics* (New York: W.H. Freeman, 1966), p. 188.

2. Ilya Prigogine and Isabelle Stengers, *Order out of Chaos*, (New York: Bantam Books, 1984), p. 217.

3. John Maynard Keynes wrote: "Ricardo conquered England as completely as the Holy Inquisition conquered Spain." See *The General Theory of Employment, Interest and Money* (London: Macmillan, 1951), p. 32.

4. Bertrand Russell, *The ABC of Relativity* (London: Allen & Unwin, 1958, 1969), p. 16.

5. A. d'Abro, *The Revolution of Scientific Thought: From Newton to Einstein*, 2nd ed. (New York: Dover Publications, 1950), p. 462.

6. Nigel Calder, *Einstein's Universe* (New York: Viking Penguin, 1979), p. 13.

7. Russell, *The ABC of Relativity*, p. 22.

8. In 1881 two American physicists, A.A. Michelson and E.W. Morley conducted the famous experiment on the constant velocity of light. For short, readable accounts of their experiments, see Lincoln Barnett, *The Universe and Dr. Einstein* (New York: New American Library, 1984), and Martin Gardner, *The Relativity Explosion* (New York: Vintage Books, 1979).

9. Eric Chaisson, *Relatively Speaking: Relativity, Black Holes, and the Fate of the Universe* (New York: W.W. Norton, 1988), pp. 56–57.

10. Prigogine and Stengers, *Order out of Chaos*, p. 218.

11. Bertrand Russell, *The ABC of Relativity*, pp. 22–23.

12. Ibid., p. 47.

13. Albert Einstein, *Relativity: The Special and General Theory—A Popular Exposition by the Author*, trans. by Robert W. Lawson (New York: Crown Publishers, 1916), p. 13.

14. Ibid., p. 34. The derivation of equation (8) is as follows: substituting equation (5) into equations (1) and (4), we have:

$$(6) \qquad x' = (ct - vt)/\sqrt{(1 - v^2/c^2)} = (c - v)t/\sqrt{(1 - v^2/c^2)}$$

$$(7) \qquad t' = (t - vct/c^2)/\sqrt{(1 - v^2/c^2)} = (1 - v/c)t/\sqrt{(1 - v^2/c^2)}$$

By division, i.e., dividing equation (6) by equation (7)—

$$x'/t' = (c - v)t/(1 - v/c)t = (c - v)/(1 - v/c) = c$$

we obtain equation (8):

$$x' = ct'.$$

15. These are the words of K.R. Atkins, *Physics* (New York: John Wiley, 1965), p. 467.

16. Morris Kline, *Mathematics in Western Culture* (New York: Oxford University Press, 1964), pp. 429–30.

17. Russell, *The ABC of Relativity*, p. 90.

18. Stephen W. Hawking, *A Brief History of Time,* (New York: Bantam Books, 1988) p. 29.

19. Paul Davies, *Other Worlds* (New York: Simon & Schuster, 1980), p. 97.

20. Quoted in ibid., p. 50.

21. Einstein, *Relativity*, p. 97.

22. F.S.C. Northrop's Introduction to Werner Heisenberg, *Physics and Philosophy* (New York: Harper & Row, 1958), p. 4.

23. Ibid., pp. 3–4.

24. Henry Margenau, "Einstein's Conception of Reality," in Paul Arthur Schlipp, ed., *Albert Einstein: Philosopher-Scientist* (New York: Harper & Row, 1959), p. 253.

25. Werner Heisenberg, *Physics and Philosophy* (New York: Harper & Row, 1958), pp. 198–99.

26. Morris Kline, *Mathematics in Western Culture*, p. 450.

27. Sir James Jeans, *Philosophy and Physics* (Ann Arbor: University of Michigan Press, 1966), p. 213.

28. Ibid., p. 213.

29. David Bohm, *Wholeness and the Implicate Order* (London: Ark Paperbacks, 1983), p. 123.

30. Ibid., pp. 124–25.

31. Quoted by Dugald Murdoch, *Niels Bohr's Philosophy of Physics* (Cambridge: Cambridge University Press, 1987), p. 195.

32. Hans Reichenbach, "The Philosophical Significance of the Theory of Relativity," in Paul Arthur Schlipp, ed., *Albert Einstein*, p. 309.

33. Ibid., p. 309.

34. Russell, *The ABC of Relativity*, pp. 138–44.

35. John Maynard Keynes, *The General Theory*, pp. 16–17. The second postulate of the classical doctrine in Keynes's words is: "The utility of the wage when a given volume of labor is employed is equal to the marginal disutility of that amount of employment" (p. 5).

36. The advocates of "post-Keynesian" economics have been called by various names, such as "neo-Keynesians," "neo-Ricardians," and the "Anglo-Italian School." The writers of this school prefer to be called "post-Keynesians." Some of the leading figures are J. Robinson, N. Kaldor, L. Pasinetti, D.M.M. Nuti, P. Sraffa, G.C. Harcourt, J.A. Kregel, P. Garegnani, A. Bhaduri, S. Weintraub, P. Davidson, E.J. Nell, and A.S. Eichner.

37. Joan Robinson, *Economic Philosophy* (Chicago: Aldine, 1962), p. 76.

38. Hans Reichenbach, "Philosophical Significance," p. 305.

39. A. d'Abro, *The Evolution of Scientific Thought*, p. 202.

40. See Philip Mirowski, *Against Mechanism* (Totowa, NJ: Roman & Littlefield, 1988); Fritjof Capra, *The Turning Point* (New York: Bantam Books, 1983); Hazel Henderson, *Creating Alternative Futures* (New York: Putnam, 1978); Prigogine and Stengers, *Order out of Chaos*; Erich Jantsch, *The Self-Organizing Universe* (Oxford: Pergamon Press, 1980); and Benjamin Ward, *What's Wrong with Economics?* (New York: Basic Books, 1972).

Chapter 5

Quantum Mechanics, Philosophy, and Economics

Students of economics generally realize that Keynes's General Theory reduces "classical" economics to a special case of full-employment equilibrium which is a limiting point of the possible position of equilibrium.[1] In physics, Einstein's introduction in his special theory of relativity of a new universal constant, c (the constant speed of light), also reduces classical physics to a special case when c is given a value of infinity (∞). The relationship between classical mechanics and quantum mechanics is similar to the above-mentioned two cases. If Planck's constant, h, is given a value of zero, all the distinctions between classical mechanics and quantum mechanics would become fuzzy.

For students of economics, the first point to know is the difference between quantum theory and quantum mechanics. Following Werner Heisenberg, quantum mechanics is the precise mathematical formulation of the original quantum theory which lacked a consistent and coherent theory of mechanics.[2] By 1925, the theory seemed to have many thorny problems. Since Max Planck's suggestion in 1900 that radiant energy emitted from a heated body in discontinuous portions that he termed quanta, believers in classical physics had deemed quantum theory irrational. They could not accept the implication of the quantum leap that the transition between stationary states is discrete. Thus Niels Bohr invoked his "correspondence principle" which "expresses [quantum theorists'] endeavors to utilize all the classical concepts by giving them a suitable quantum-theoretical re-interpretation."[3] The fervent hope of Bohr was materialized when his assistant Werner Heisenberg discovered a new mathematical formalism that has come to be known as "quantum mechanics" or "matrix mechanics." Quantum theory was resuscitated. Bohr called this new breakthrough "the creation of rational quantum mechanical methods."[4] Heisenberg's "matrix mechanics" was subsequently further developed by Max Born and Pascual Jordan.

To keep the explanation of the mathematical formalism simple and manageable for our purpose, we attempt to give an informal exposition of operators calculus instead of matrices. The justification for taking this approach is that operators calculus is related to the mathematics of matrices. The rules governing the use of matrices are the same as the mathematical rules used to handle operators.

What is an operator? An operator is any symbol or letter that indicates that an agreed process has to be carried out; this process will change a mathematical function in a definite way. For example, suppose we have a function x^2 and the operator is d/dx. The function x^2 is thus changed to $2x$ through the differentiating process, $dx^2/dx = 2x$, where $2x$ is called the eigenfunction of the operator d/dx; the number 2 is called the eigenvalue of the operator. For each operator there is a corresponding ensemble of numerical values. This ensemble forms the operator's "spectrum." If the eigenvalues are a discrete series, such as $(0, 1, 2, \ldots, n)$, then the "spectrum" is also discrete.

It is rather astonishing to note that the order in which one operator acts on another one makes a great deal of difference. For example, if the operators are represented by the letters A and B (both could be interpreted as matrices), the results A times B and B times A are not the same ($A{\cdot}B \neq B{\cdot}A$). The most lucid numerical illustration of this strange result is given by Fred Alan Wolf:

Operators are also capable of being operated upon. Thus the operator called "square" can be multiplied by any number, say 3. . . . This makes "3 times square" a new operator. When "3 times square" operates upon "5," it makes 75 instead of 25. . . . But "square times 3" operating on "5" gives the result of multiplying 3 times 5 and then squaring. This gives 225, instead.[5]

In the language of operators calculus, the strange phenomenon— i.e., $A \cdot B \neq B \cdot A$—means that the two operators do not commute.

The above-mentioned mathematics had been applied by quantum theorists to the classical Hamiltonian function. As we stated at the end of chapter 1, the Hamiltonian function, H, is expressed in terms of position (coordinates) and velocity (momentum). A single function $H(p,q)$ describes the dynamics of any system completely, where p stands for coordinates and q depicts momentum. In quantum mechanics, p and q are treated as operators. Since operators in quantum theory do not commute, the profound implication of this phenomenon is that one cannot identify a function that would be an eigenfunction for both p and q, whereas in classical dynamics, both p and q could have well-defined values simultaneously. In the language of quantum mechanics, p and q are commuting operators. This assumption is reflected in the canonical equations of the optimal neoclassical growth model presented in chapter 1. The canonical equations stated therein are: $\delta H/\delta k = - \dot{\mu}$ and $\delta H/\delta \mu = \dot{k}$. It is evident that μ and k do commute. In the quantum mechanics case, there can be no state in which both p and q could have well-defined values simultaneously. This led to Heisenberg's principle of uncertainty, or indeterminacy, which will be considered later in this chapter.

Main Features of Quantum Mechanics

The history of quantum mechanics is very complex. Since it is our intention to show the interrelations between economics, philosophy, and physics, we think it will be useful for students of economics to have an understanding of certain main features of this revolutionary theory.

The Inherent Wholeness of Atomic Process

The prevailing scientific view of the natural world before the work of Max Planck may be summarized as follows: material objects were explained in terms of particles, and electromagnetic radiation (including light) was described in terms of waves. In 1900 Max Planck succeeded in giving a complete explanation of the matter-light radiation interaction by introducing the formula: $E = h\upsilon$, where E stands for the radiant energy emitted from a heated body in discontinuous bits which he termed "quanta" (which means wholeness); the Greek letter *nu*, υ, depicts the frequency of the radiation; and h, which measures the size of each quantum leap, is the new universal constant generally known as Planck's constant, which has since proven to be one of the most fundamental constants in nature.

One of the far-reaching effects of Planck's constant, as pointed out by Prigogine and Stengers,[6] is to reduce the number of independent variables of classical mechanics. In the classical Hamiltonian system, p and q are independent variables. If one looks at the Einstein-de Broglie equations: $\mu = h/p$, or $p = h\mu$ (which will be considered in the following sections), one will notice that wave length, signified by the Greek letter μ (length is closely related to coordinates or position), and momenta denoted by the letter p, are connected by Planck's constant h. Hence position and momentum can no longer be independent variables as in the classical Hamiltonian system. One can only know the quantity of either p or q, but not both simultaneously. This is another notion that lends support to Heisenberg's principle of indeterminacy or uncertainty. As so aptly stated by Paul Davies, "To the quantum physicist the universe is an inseparable web of vibrating energy patterns in which no one component has reality independently of the entirety; and included in the observer."[7] In other words, the universe is a network of relations. Although the numerical value of Planck's h is very small (6.63 times 10^{-34} joule seconds), yet the macroscopic and microscopic worlds are interwoven. Even though the quantum effect is only conspicuous in the atomic and subatomic realm, one must not forget that the world is ultimately a collection of quantum mechanical systems. This is analogous to the microfoundations of macroeconomics. Our macroeconomic theories would be standing on shifting sands if they did not have firm microfoundations.

The impact of Planck's constant can also be seen in Niels Bohr's studies in the quantum model of the atom, Einstein's theory of the "wave-particle duality" of light, and the evolution of "wave mechanics" of Louis de Broglie, Irwin Schrodinger, and Max Born.

Niels Bohr interpreted Planck's h as a unit of angular momentum (which can be thought of as tethered momentum moving in a circle around a reference point). Bohr's electron was orbiting about the nucleus. It was tethered to the reference point, namely the nucleus, by the electrical attraction between the electron and the nucleus inside an atom. In the words of Fred Alan Wolf, "By allowing the electron to have only whole units of h and not any other amounts of angular momentum, Bohr discovered the rule that kept the electron in a stable orbit."[8] While the electron was orbiting peacefully inside an atom, it did not radiate light. Only when the electron makes the "quantum leap" from one orbit to another will it radiate light. Thus Bohr brought Einstein's "wave-particle duality of light" into his quantum model of the atom in 1913, eight years after Einstein's discovery.

It is ironic that Einstein, who refused to accept the statistical nature of quantum mechanics,[9] was the first distinguished physicist to embrace Planck's constant. In 1905 Einstein suggested that all forms of radiant energy, such as heat, light, etc., travel through space in discontinuous quanta. He postulated that electromagnetic radiation consists of streams of photons and that photon energy was represented by $h\upsilon$ of Planck's equation, $E = h\upsilon$. This interpretation has been known as Einstein's photoelectric effect. An important dynamical property of the photon is the relation between energy (E) and momentum (p), which is described by the equation, $E = cp$, where the letter c is Einstein's universal constant, namely the constant velocity of light. Rearranging the symbols of the equation $E = cp$, we obtain $p = E/c$. Substituting $h\upsilon$ for E in the new equation, we get the relation, $p = h\upsilon/c$, or $c = h\upsilon/p$. The equation for the wavelength of light is $\mu = c/\upsilon$, which may be rewritten as $c = \mu\upsilon$. Since Einstein's universal constant, c, is the link between the equations, $p = h\upsilon/c$ and $c = \mu\upsilon$, one can write $h\upsilon/p = \mu\upsilon$. When we divide both sides of the new relation by υ, we get the Louis de Broglie equation, $\mu = h/p$.

In 1924 Louis de Broglie extended Einstein's "wave-particle duality of light" to "wave-particle duality of matter." The de Broglie equation $\mu = h/p$ may be written as $p\mu = h$. Since h is constant, the equation implies that the larger the momentum of a particle, the smaller its wavelength will be. This means that electrons, with their small mass and corresponding small momentum (p), are the most "wavelike" among particles.

In 1926 Irwin Schrodinger presented his "wave mechanics" by a mathematical formula that explained the changing wave patterns inside an atom. Unlike his contemporary Heisenberg, probability and uncertainty did not seem to enter his high-power mathematics. Schrodinger appears to have been working for the preservation of the classical approach of continuous mathematical description. Later in the same year, Max Born stressed that Schrodinger's wave function should not be thought of as representing electrons. Rather, the wave function should be related to the probability of finding an electron in space. In this way the Schrodinger wave function is compatible with Heisenberg's uncertainty principle. As David Bohm points out: "The fundamental laws of the quantum theory are to be expressed with the aid of a wave function."[10] Following Bohm, if the wave function is given as follows:

$$\Phi = \sum_n C_n \Phi_n$$

where Φ_n is the eigenfunction of the operator in question corresponding to the nth eigenvalue, the probability of obtaining the nth eigenvalue in a large ensemble of measurements will be given by $P_n = |C_n|^2$. To extract information on the desired observable from the statistical wave function, the physicist needs certain operators that operate linearly on the given wave function. The desired observable will be sharply defined only if the given wave function is an eigenfunction of the corresponding operator. We have already mentioned that many operators do not commute, and, in Bohm's words, "It follows that no wave functions can exist which are simultaneous eigenfunctions of all operators that are significant for a given physical problem. This means that not all physically significant observables can be determined together, and even more important, that those which are not determined will fluctuate lawlessly (at random) in a series of measurements on an ensemble represented by the same wave function."[11]

It is evident that despite the differences between Schrodinger's "wave mechanics" and the "matrix mechanics" of Heisenberg and associates, the mathematical formulations of both will produce identical results. It is also important to note that the "fuzzy" quantum mechanics actually provide an elaborate mathematical framework, as Paul Davies puts it, that holds together most of the modern physics: "Without quantum mechanics our detailed and extensive understanding of atoms, nuclei, molecules [e.g., DNA], crystals, light, electricity, subatomic particles, lasers, transistors, and much else would disintegrate."[12] Michio Kaku and Jennifer Trainer in the same vein also observe:

> Although the Schrodinger wave function is difficult to solve for increasingly complicated atoms and molecules, we could, if we had a large enough computer, deduce the properties of all known chemicals from first principle . . . it also allows us to calculate the properties of chemicals that we have yet to see in nature.[13]

The inherent wholeness of the quantum process is further highlighted by what Bohm called "nonlocality."[14] By "nonlocality,'' he is referring to the difference between classical physics and quantum mechanics. In classical physics the basic constituent parts of the universe are independent of the whole system. Newton's universal law of gravitation postulates that every particle of matter in the universe attracts every other particle with a force (F) varying directly proportional to the product of the masses (M_1M_2) and inversely as the square of distance between them (R^2) (see chapter 1). It implies that the locality of the particles determines the strength of the force of gravitation. In other words, the clockwork of the mechanistic universe hinges on the ''local mechanism.'' In the quantum world, Bohm stressed that ''the system cannot be analyzed into parts. . . . This leads to the radically new notion of unbroken wholeness of the entire universe.''[15] The ''nonlocality'' quantum phenomenon had been confirmed by the experiments of Alain Aspect in 1981 and 1982. These experiments were designed to determine the extent of correlation between the photon under observation and the measurement of the other photon. The results are succinctly summarized by Paul Davies:

> The two particle arrangement described in the foregoing reveals that the reality of a particle ''over there'' is indissolubly linked with the reality of a particle ''over here.'' The simplistic assumption that just because two particles have moved a long way apart we can consider them as separate and independent physical entities is badly wrong. . . . The non-local aspect of quantum systems is therefore a general property of nature, and not just a freak situation manufactured in the laboratory.[16]

In the same vein, one should not consider the ''Butterfly Effect'' of weather forecast as a ''half-joke.''[17]

The Copenhagen Interpretation of Quantum Mechanics

The ''Copenhagen Interpretation'' marked the completion of the consistent quantum theory. First presented by Niels Bohr in

1927, the concept is represented by the following cluster of ideas: (a) statistical wave mechanics (considered in the preceding sections); (b) Heinsenberg's principle of indeterminacy (or uncertainty); and (c) Bohr's principle of complementarity. The two latter ideas are elucidated in this section.

The inherent fuzziness of quantum mechanics prompted Heisenberg in 1927 to suggest the principle of indeterminacy, which stated that the position of the electron (p) and its momentum (q) cannot have precise values simultaneously. The uncertainty relation is written as:

$$\Delta q \Delta p \approx h$$

where Δq denotes the degree of uncertainty of all electrons' positions; Δp stands for the degree of uncertainty of an electron's momentum; the sign $\approx$ means that the value of the product ($\Delta q \Delta p$) is not very different from that of h, which is, of course, Planck's constant. Since the numerical value of h is very small, the quantum fuzziness is only conspicuous in the atomic and subatomic realm. Heisenberg postulated that in the subatomic world the process of taking a measurement of an atomic system disturbs the system and changes it qualitatively. Michio Kaku and Jennifer Trainer explain Heisenberg's proposition as follows: "An electron is so small that to measure its positions in an atom, photons of light must be bounced off it. However, the light is so powerful that it bumps the electron out of the atom, changing the electron's position and location."[18]

Heisenberg's idea that to observe is to disturb has been invoked by the economist Kenneth Boulding to spotlight the ethical component of social sciences:

> My favorite illustration of the Heisenberg principle is the story of a man who inquires through the door of the bedroom where his friend is sick. "How are you?" whereupon the friend replies, "Fine," and the effort kills him. In the social sciences of course the generalized

> Heisenberg principle predominates; knowledge of the social sciences is an essential part of the social system itself; hence objectivity in the sense of investigating a world which is unchanged by the investigation of it is an absurdity.[19]

The implication of Heisenberg's famous principle is that the properties of the electron are inseparable from the experimenter and his measuring apparatus. In other words, the physicist can choose to measure either position or momentum of an electron precisely. However, the more precisely the position is measured, the more fuzzy the momentum becomes. One can see this implication from Heisenberg's equation, $\Delta q \Delta p \approx h$. Since h is constant, the reduction of Δp can be brought about at the expense of a larger Δq, and vice versa.

The principle of indeterminacy also applies to energy (E) and time (t). In this case, Heisenberg's fundamental equation would be: $\Delta E \Delta t \approx h$, which implies that uncertainty in time (Δt) can only be reduced at the expense of a large uncertainty in energy (ΔE). The explanation for this phenomenon is that the energy of a photon is directly proportional to the frequency of light. Therefore, a physicist can measure energy through the measurement of the frequency of the light wave. In other words, the experimenter can count the number of peaks and troughs of the wave that pass by in a given interval of time. For visible light, the time duration involved is very short. If the duration is shorter than one cycle of the wave, the energy will be exceedingly difficult to determine precisely. What is important, as Paul Davies points out, is that the energy-time uncertainty relation, like that of the position-momentum, is not restricted to photons but applies to all subatomic activity.[20]

The principle of complementarity was presented by Niels Bohr at a lecture in Como, Italy in 1927. The salient points of the principle are: (a) Both wave and particle aspects are necessary to understand the quantum world. According to Bohr, all those incompatibilities, such as wave-particle duality and position-momentum indeterminacy, are complementary aspects of a single reality.

(b) Which aspect of the quantum object is presented to us depends upon the choice of the physicists and upon their choice of measuring apparatus. All the observer knows are the results of experiments. As so aptly stated by Bruce Gregory: "Physicists do not discover the physical world, they invent a physical world—they invent a story that fits closely as possible the facts they create in their experimental apparatus."[21] According to Bohr, "the word 'reality' is also a word, a word we must learn to use correctly."[22] To the question posed by Fred Alan Wolf: "Is there an 'out there' there?" the answer given by quantum physicists probably would be: "Reality is a matter of Choice."

In other words, the principle of complementarity emphasizes the importance of experiments in our understanding of the quantum world. The question of what the electrons are doing when the physicist is not looking at them is not meaningful because the physicist can only make meaningful statements about the condition of an electron within the context of a specific experimental arrangement. This point leads to an important and seemingly paradoxical implication, namely, the quantum microworld and the classical (nonquantum) macroworld are actually very closely interrelated. The reason is that the measuring apparatus and the experimenters must first exist in the macroworld before quantum properties such as the position and momentum of an electron can have any precise meaning. In the words of David Bohm, "large-scale and small-scale properties are both needed to describe complementary aspects of a more fundamentally indivisible unit, namely, the system as a whole."[23] In a similar vein, Paul Davies writes: "There is thus a sort of circularity involved: the macro-world needs the micro-world to constitute it and the micro-world needs the macro-world to define it . . . [for] the act of measurement transforms probability into certainty by projecting out or selecting a specific result from among a range of possibilities."[24] In the case of the Max Born-Schrodinger statistical wave function, the results of the experiment have been called by physicists the "collapse of the wave function."[25]

The Post–Copenhagen-Interpretation Synthesis

After 1927, quantum mechanics had been formulated in such a form, as pointed out by John Gribbin, that "would be used by any competent physicist to solve problems involving atoms and molecules with no great need for thought about fundamentals but a single willingness to follow the recipe book and turn out the answers."[26] In the words of Richard P. Feynman, "The theory of quantum mechanics explained all kinds of details, such as why an oxygen atom combines with two hydrogen atoms to make water, and so on. Quantum mechanics thus supplied the theory behind chemistry. So the fundamental theoretical chemistry is really physics."[27]

Quantum theory, however, did not score a total victory, for quantum mechanics can only explain the behavior of particles whose speed is slower than the speed of light, such as lasers and transistors. Particles with speed faster than that of light would be the unreachable stars for quantum mechanics. To be a complete theory, quantum mechanics has to incorporate the theory of relativity. Hence the synthesis of relativity and quantum theories became the "Holy Grail" sought by quantum crusaders for the past fifty years or so. Richard P. Feynman observes:

> Because the theory of quantum mechanics could explain all of chemistry and the various properties of substances, it was a tremendous success. But still there was the problem of the interaction of light and matter. That is, Maxwell's theory of electricity and magnetism had to be changed to be in accord with the new principles of quantum mechanics that had been developed. So a new theory, the quantum theory of the interaction of light and matter, which is called by the horrible name "quantum electrodynamics," was finally developed by a number of physicists in 1929.[28]

The "horrible name" has been abbreviated as "QED." The Feynman formulation of QED is the most successful model of modern physics.

There was, broadly speaking, a parallel development in the

discipline of economics. After the initial conquest of the "Keynesian Revolution," the economics profession began to look inward to consider the issue of the microfoundations of Keynesian macroeconomics. In 1939 John Hicks made a breakthrough by developing essentially a Walrasian general equilibrium analysis without the "auctioneer." From 1939 to 1956, the economics profession witnessed rapid progress in the clearing of conceptual underbrush and in the sharpening of analytical tools. In 1947 Samuelson introduced his "correspondence principle," which clarified certain ambiguities in comparative statics. In early 1950s, Kenneth J. Arrow, Gerard Debreu, and other distinguished mathematical economists completed rigorous proofs of the existence of competitive equilibria. In 1956 Don Patinkin integrated monetary and value theory within the neo-Walrasian general equilibrium framework. These economists' concerted efforts brought about the "golden age" of the so-called "neoclassical synthesis"—a synthesis of Keynesian and neo-Walrasian general equilibrium theories—which dominated the paradigm of economic science from the 1950s to the beginning of the 1970s.[29]

Whereas the neoclassical synthesis began to falter after the vigorous criticisms launched by the post-Keynesians,[30] the quest for unity by quantum physicists made remarkable advances in the 1960s. One of the important contributing factors to that success story was the dramatic developments in the area of high-energy particle physics on both the experimental and the conceptual levels.

The subatomic world, in terms of matter, was relatively simple before 1927. Physicists during that period knew that all matter is the same on earth as well as in heaven. There is nothing but atoms, which have nuclei and around the nuclei there are electrons. But the high-energy particle collision experiments opened a Pandora's box. More than four dozen new particles have been discovered. Fortunately, these new particles come in families which helps to simplify problems a great deal. Richard P. Feynman gives the following simplified family tree of the particles:[31]

electrons	neutrons
photons	protons
	(+ over four dozen more)
neutrinos	
mu mesons (muons)	
mu neutrinos	
gravitons	
(+ all anti-particles)	

Neutrons and protons are the two components of nuclei. Photons are particles of light. From quantum mechanics, gravitation has some kind of waves that can also behave like particles. Such "particles" are called "gravitons." Not all particles carry electric charges. Photons and neutrinos are electrically neutral. Neutrinos are ghostly particles, in the words of Paul Davies, "that have no mass and travel at the speed of light. So insubstantial are neutrinos that they can easily pass right through the earth. . . . Countless millions of them are passing through you as you read these words."[32] But the real significance of photons and neutrinos, as we shall see, is that they serve as "messenger" particles.

Following Paul Davies,[33] the sources of change in nature can be attributed to four fundamental forces: (1) gravity, (2) electromagnetism, (3) the weak force, and (4) the strong force. The strong force binds the protons together against the repulsion caused by their electronic charges. Both neutrons and protons are subject to strong forces. Electrons, neutrinos, and photons are not affected by strong forces. Particles subject to the strong forces are called hadrons. Inside all hadrons are small particles called quarks which either stick together in trio or in quark-antiquark pairs. Neutrons and protons belong to the "trio" groups; the quark-antiquark groupings are called "mesons." Particles that are subject to weak forces are called "leptons." The best-known leptons are electrons and neutrinos.

In Feynman's formulation of QED, forces are subsumed under the interaction of particles in the "quantum field." In the concept of "quantum field" one perceives the synthesis of Einstein's relativity theory and quantum mechanics. From the theory of Einstein, QED incorporates the concept that photons are electromagnetic waves in electromagnetic fields. From the Einstein-de Broglie hypothesis of "wave-particle duality," QED suggests the "field theory of matter," which destroys the classical belief in solid particles separated from the space surrounding them. Hermann Weyl points out that:

> According to the field theory of matter a material particle such as an electron is merely a small domain of the electrical field within which the field strength assumes enormously high values, indicating that a comparatively huge field energy is concentrated in a very small space. Such an energy knot, which by no means is clearly delineated against the remaining field, propagates through empty space like a water wave across the surface of [a] lake; there is no such thing as one and the same substance of which the electron consists at all times.[34]

The "field theory of matter" is interwoven with what Paul Davies calls "the living vacuum."[35] This new hypothesis is inspired by Heisenberg's principle of uncertainty as it relates to the behavior of energy. It will be recalled that the Heisenberg equation relating to energy and time is: $Et \approx h$. When t is very short, as Davies points out, energy can be "borrowed" for all manner of purposes, one of which is to create particles. But the newly created particles have only a fleeting existence before they fade once again into oblivion. However, in view of the Heisenberg loan process, "what might appear to be empty space, is, therefore, a seething ferment of virtual particles. A vacuum is not inert and featureless, but alive with throbbing energy and vitality."[36]

In Feynman's QED, the interaction between two electrons in the "living vacuum" is illustrated by Figure 5.1:

Figure 5.1. **A Feynman diagram showing the interaction between two electrons through a photon, the messenger particle**

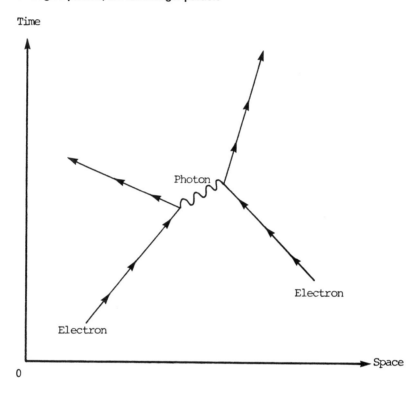

Several points need further explanation. First, in the search for synthesis, the Einsteinian space-time diagram was incorporated by Feynman in the 1940s. Feynman, however, introduced the new idea that the world lines of the electrons could move backward in time (this is one of Feynman's innovations for the purpose of removing the vexed problem of ''infinities,'' discussion of which is beyond the scope of this book). This changing of direction is depicted by the link of the two world lines. Second, the messenger particle, the photon, is the carrier of the electric field. Hence, it is of crucial importance in the description of particle behavior. Third, theoretically, electrons are surrounded by ''virtual'' photons. As electrons are continually released, they become messenger particles. The path of a messenger particle is depicted by the wavy line in Figure 5.1. The photon is absorbed by the other electron at point B. Consequently, the world line of the second electron changes its direction. Says Davies, "Messenger photons have been compared with the ball that is exchanged between tennis players. Just as a tennis ball shapes the pattern of activity followed by the players, so the photons influence the behavior of the electrons."[37]

The fourth and most important point is that, in their unceasing research in formulating a comprehensive synthesis of relativity and quantum theories, physicists have acquired a remarkable insight into the fundamental unity of knowledge. The new insight is the perception of the hitherto only vaguely recognized interrelations among several fundamental laws of nature: (a) the connection between conservation laws and symmetry laws; (b) the relationship between symmetry laws and relativity theory; (c) the dependence of QED and the laws of symmetry; and (d) the relationship between symmetry laws and the forces of nature.

Richard P. Feynman points out that, "It is extremely interesting that there seems to be a deep connection between conservation laws and the symmetry laws. This connection has its proper interpretation only in the knowledge of quantum mechanics . . . but that connection requires that the minimum principle be assumed."[38] Feynman's insight is best illustrated by Paul Davies's analogy of strollers in the park and the seemingly chaotic behavior of subatomic particles,[39] paraphrased as follows: Consider a small park with a fence around it and two gates on opposite sides. Suppose the small park is situated on some frequently used thoroughfare. People who walk across it are not subject to any rigid law of motion. Many of them may stray away from the shortest route. However, when a sufficiently large group of people using the park is studied, it is highly probable that there will be a concentration of paths near the shortest route. The shortest route in the analogy implies the path of least action, or Feynman's "minimum principle." It also refers to the law of symmetry for it is the path most likely to be followed by the pedestrians. Hence, the "minimum principle" is also conserved. The strollers in the park behave like subatomic particles. Electrons, for instance, would also "choose" a whole variety of paths, although the ones they prefer are the low-action ones. (Bertrand Russell called this "cosmic laziness.") However, it is all a matter of probability. Therefore it cannot be explained by the deterministic Newtonian physics. It can only be properly interpreted by quantum mechanics.

The connection between the laws of conservation and Einstein's special theory of relativity is plain to see. We may recall that the first fundamental principle of the special theory states that all inertial frames are equivalent with respect to all laws of physics. "Inertial frames" means that the terms of reference are confined to those motions with uniform velocity in straight lines. In the language of symmetry laws, "inertial frames" refers to "global gauge symmetries." In QED most of the symmetries considered are called "logical gauge symmetries," which means the invariance of laws of physics under arbitrary changes in the shape of paths of motion. The word "gauge" is sometimes used to describe the distance between the rails of a railway. When physicists talk about "gauge field," they consider it as a "force field" similar to "electromagnetic field" or "gravitational field." The function of the gauge field is to keep the laws of physics (analogous to the moving train) on track under sudden arbitrary changes in the shape of a path of motion. In QED, the messenger particles, photons, are carriers of the electromagnetic field. Hence they are sometimes called "gauge particles," since their frantic activities do not alter the identities of the interacting electrons. In this sense, the identities of the interacting electrons are conserved, even though their paths of motion have altered after the interaction.

It should be noted that gauge symmetries are not the same as the more familiar geometrical symmetries such as reflection-symmetries of human features in a mirror. Gauge symmetries are "abstract" in the same sense as is the index-linked income device under conditions of rising price inflation in economics. Index-linked income is gauge-symmetric in the conservation of the real purchasing power of money income (or "re-gauging" of money).

Maintaining local gauge symmetries in nature requires the unification of the four forces of nature. This is the new insight acquired by physicists in their attempts to unite the four forces into a common "superforce" (which is outside of the scope of this book).

Quantum Mechanics and Economics

The most explicit statement of the impact of quantum mechanics on economics was made by Kenneth E. Boulding in his presidential address delivered to the American Economic Association, Chicago, December 29, 1968:

> The notion that science is simply discovering knowledge about an objectively unchangeable world may have some validity in the early stages of science, but as sciences have developed it has become less and less valid. The learning process of science is now running into two serious difficulties.[40]

The first serious difficulty Boulding calls "the generalized Heisenberg principle." According to this principle, "when we try to obtain knowledge about a system by changing its inputs and outputs of information, the new inputs and outputs will change the system itself and under certain circumstances change it radically."[41] His favorite illustration of the principle was the story of the sick friend and the visitor which we already quoted.

The second serious difficulty stressed by Boulding is that "as science develops, it no longer merely investigates the world; it creates the world it is investigating."[42] Hence Boulding emphasized that what science (including economic science) creates becomes a problem of ethical choice; and "the whole future of science may well rest on our ability to resolve the ethical conflicts which the growth of knowledge is now creating."[43]

Although, as far as we know, other economists do not explicitly mention the influence of quantum mechanics, the inherent wholeness of the quantum process has contributed to the revived interests of a number of writers in attacking the reductionist methodology of orthodox economics. In an increasingly interrelated world today, quite a few economists, thinking that the systems approach is essential for understanding our modern economic problems, are calling for a paradigm shift. The most ardent advocates of the systems approach are the alternative-futurists, such as E.F. Schumacher, Hazel Henderson, and others.[44] The following view, expressed by Hazel Henderson, is representative of the tenets of that school of thought: "Speaking of our current series of crises, Henderson affirms: 'Whether we designate them as 'energy crises,' 'environmental crises,' 'urban crises,' or 'population crises,' we should recognize the extent to which they are all rooted in the larger crisis of our inadequate, narrow perceptions of reality.' ''[45]

The antideterminist and statistical nature of quantum mechanics has a "shadow influence" on modern post-Keynesian economists. One of the tenets of the post-Keynesians is their emphasis on uncertainty and a nonergodic world. For example, Paul Davidson's excellent book, *Money and the Real World*, contains a perceptive consideration of uncertainty in a monetary economy.[46] The "shadow influence" of quantum mechanics may also be seen in Davidson's critique of the rational expectations hypothesis. In an essay entitled "Rational Expectations: A Fallacious Foundation for Studying Crucial Decision-Making Processes,"[47] Davidson points out that the stochastic process envisaged by the theorists of rational expectations is stationary and ergotic. Davidson favors the arguments of Keynes, Hicks, and G.L.S. Shackle that real-world economic situations are nonergotic. The "shadow influence" of quantum mechanics may also be behind the writings of some economists of non-post-Keynesian persuasion.[48]

Quantum Mechanics and Philosophy

One of the important philosophical implications of the Copenhagen interpretation of quantum mechanics is on the question of realism. According to Dugald Murdoch,[49] Niels Bohr clearly rejected scientific realism, by which Murdoch means a particularly strong form of realism. "On this view," writes Murdoch, "atoms and elementary particles exist, but in reality there are no such things as the physical objects—such as tables and chairs—conceived of by common sense."[50] Bohr, on the contrary, holds that the common-sense conception of physical reality is not entirely wrong. But it is not complete. "For Bohr the two conceptions of physical reality, namely, the common-sense and the quantum-physical, are not incompatible but complementary, and hence appropriate to different points of view or modes of apprehension."[51] This is the philosophy behind Bohr's principles of "correspondence" and "complementarity" which we considered earlier in this chapter.

Murdoch points out that Bohr is attracted to Soren Kierkegaard's view of reality, according to which reality can be "fully comprehended only from different points of view or in terms of disparate conceptual schemes."[52] Bohr's view opened the Pandora's box of speculations on the nature and existence of reality, or even its very meaningfulness, or the extent to which quantum features may have undermined it. "Nevertheless," says Paul Davies, "certain problems and paradoxes have been tossed around for fifty years or so, and although they are not resolved to everyone's satisfaction, they highlight the profoundly strange qualities that quantum theory has brought into our world."[53]

In the earlier stages of quantum mechanics, the question of the "collapse of the wave function" implied that there was no single reality. This problem was illustrated by the Irwin Schrodinger's well-known cat paradox. Schrodinger, like Einstein, did not find the implications of quantum mechanics acceptable; he introduced the "cat paradox" with a view to showing the absurdity of those implications. This paradox has been succinctly explained by Paul Davies: "Schrodinger envisaged a cat incarcerated in a box with a flask of cyanide gas. The box also contains a radioactive source and a Geiger counter that can trigger a hammer to smash the flask if a nucleus decays. . . . The cat is apparently hung up in a hybrid state of unreality in which it is somehow both dead and alive!'' The state of unreality ends when the observer opens the box to see the state of the cat.[54] In Davies's view,[55] subsequent attempts to meet the challenge of the paradox fall into two categories: First, there are those who accept the universal validity of the implications of quantum mechanics and adhere to the theory of many worlds. Second, there are those who no longer consider the fuzziness of the subatomic world as the final truth. The leading exponent of the more radical theory is David Bohm.

In *Wholeness and the Implicate Order*, David Bohm suggests a new approach to reality which goes beyond those implied by relativity and quantum theories. The point of departure of his approach is the basically common feature of both theories, namely the notion of ''undivided wholeness'' of the universe. Bohm writes: ''Though each comes to such wholeness in a different way, it is clear that it is this to which they are both fundamentally pointing.''[56] He proposes a new notion of order, which he calls the ''implicate order.'' The Latin root of the word ''implicate'' means to ''enfold'' or to ''fold inward.'' ''In terms of the implicate order,'' Bohm points out, ''one may say that everything is enfolded into everything. This contrasts with the 'explicit order' now dominant in physics in which things are unfolded in the sense that each thing lies only in its own particular region of space and time and outside the regions belonging to other things.''[57]

Bohm suggests that the hologram may help to illustrate the new order in a perceptive way. Each part of the hologram is an image of the whole object. In other words, information about the whole is enfolded in each part of the image. Of course, Bohm emphasizes, the holograph is only a ''snapshot'' of the implicate order:

> The actual order itself is in the complex movement of electromagnetic fields, in the form of light waves. Such movement of light waves is present everywhere and in principle enfolds the entire universe of space (and time) in each region (as can be demonstrated in

such region by placing one's eye or a telescope there, which will "unfold" this content).[58]

Further, explains Bohm: "What I'm suggesting here is that the movement of enfolding and unfolding is ultimately the primary reality, and that the objects, entities, forms, and so on, which appear in this movement are secondary."[59] He calls this universal movement the "holomovement."

David Bohm met J. Krishnamurti in 1961. The quantum physicist and the Eastern philosopher became great friends. Bohm's universal "holomovement" may have been influenced by the thinking of Krishnamurti. It is interesting to note that Niels Bohr was also attracted to Eastern philosophy. In "The Unity of Human Knowledge" (1960), Bohr wrote:

> We are here confronted with complementary relationships inherent in the human position, and unforgettably expressed in old Chinese philosophy, reminding us that in the great drama of existence we are ourselves both actors and spectators.[60]

The reason for the quantum physicists' interest in Eastern philosophy is best explained by Fritjof Capra:

> In the twentieth century, physicists penetrated deep into the submicroscopic world, into realms of nature far removed form our macroscopic environment. Our knowledge of matter at this level is no longer derived from direct sensory experience, and therefore our ordinary language is no longer adequate to describe the observed phenomena. Atomic physics provided the scientists with the first glimpses of the essential nature of things. Like the mystics, physicists were now dealing with a nonsensory experience of reality and, like the mystics, they had to face the paradoxical aspects of this experience. From then on, models and images of modern physics became akin to those of Eastern philosophy.[61]

Capra's perceptive explanation has not been generally accepted by modern physicists. The reason for the impasse probably lies in a fear of losing one's commitment to science.

The inherent wholeness of atomic process also gives impetus to the emerging new paradigm of the "self-organizing" principle expounded by the so-called "Brussels School" under the leadership of Ilya Prigogine, the Nobel Prize laureate of 1977. The main ideas of the school have been succinctly summarized by Alvin Toffler as follows[62]:

(a) The Newtonian mechanistic world view concerns itself mostly with closed systems and linear relationships. But the phenomena of the high-technology industrial societies of today are open systems in which information and innovation are the critical resources. (b) All systems contain subsystems that are continually fluctuating. The order and organization of the existing system will be shattered when the fluctuations become very powerful. The critical point has been called the "bifurcation point." It is impossible to determine in advance which direction change will take. (c) In the view of Prigogine, order and organization can arise spontaneously out of chaos through a "self-organization process."

The "self-organizing principle" has introduced an optimistic "arrow of time" in the universe. Unlike the pessimistic "arrow of time" implied by the second law of thermodynamics, the universe is revealed in a new and more inspiring light.

The idea of order out of chaos is also implied by the philosophy of the late biologist Gregory Bateson. After studying Prigogine's "self-organizing principle," and discussions with Erich Jantsch (author of *The Self-Organizing Universe*[63]), Fritjof Capra asked Gregory Bateson about his insight that mind and self-organization are merely different aspects of one and the same phenomenon, the phenomenon of life. Bateson's answer was: "You are right. Mind is the essence of being alive."[64]

Other strains of thought beyond the quantum, to name a few, are Paul Davies, *The Cosmic Blueprint*, John D. Barrow and Frank J. Tipler, *The Anthropic Cosmological Principle*, and Rupert Sheldrake, *New Science of Life*. Considerations of these works are beyond the scope of this book.

Notes

1. See J.M. Keynes, *The General Theory of Employment, Interest and Money* (London: Macmillan, 1951), p. 3.

2. See Werner Heisenberg, *Physics and Philosophy* (New York: Harper & Row, 1958), pp. 38–40.

3. See Niels Bohr, *The Philosophical Writings of Niels Bohr*, vol. 1 (Woodbridge, CT: Ox Bow Press, 1987 [This is a reprint of the original 1934 publication by Cambridge University Press], p. 8. Bohr and Heisenberg were both leaders of the so-called Copenhagen School of Quantum Theory.

4. Ibid., p. 7.

5. Fred Alan Wolf, *Taking the Quantum Leap* (San Francisco: Harper & Row, 1981), p. 107.

6. Prigogine and Stengers, *Order out of Chaos* (New York: Bantam Books, 1984), pp. 222–23.

7. Paul Davies, *Superforce* (New York: Simon & Schuster, 1984), p. 49.

8. Wolf, *Taking the Quantum Leap*, p. 82.

9. In 1927 thirty or more distinguished physicists including Einstein were gathered for the fifth Solvay conference in Brussels. Niels Bohr wrote: "Einstein expressed a deep concern over the extent to which causal account in space and time was abandoned in quantum mechanics." See *The Philosophical Writings of Niels Bohr*, vol. 2 (Woodbridge, CT: Ox Bow Press, 1987), p. 41.

10. David Bohm, *Wholeness and the Implicate Order* (London: Ark Paperbacks, 1983), p. 66.

11. Ibid.

12. Paul Davies, *Other Worlds* (New York: Simon & Schuster, 1980), pp. 17–18.

13. Michio Kaku and Jennifer Trainer, *Beyond Einstein: The Cosmic Quest for the Theory of the Universe* (New York: Bantam Books, 1987), pp. 45–46.

14. David Bohm and B. Hiley, "On the Intuitive Understanding of Nonlocality as Implied by Quantum Theory," *Foundations of Physics* 5 (1975): 94. Quoted by Wolf, in *Taking the Quantum Leap*, p. 177.

15. Ibid.

16. Davies, *Superforce*, p. 48.

17. The "butterfly effect" is discussed in chapter 6.

18. Michio Kaku and Jennifer Trainer, *Beyond Einstein*, p. 49.

19. Kenneth E. Boulding, "Economics as a Moral Science," in *Economics as a Science* (New York: McGraw-Hill, 1970), p. 121.

20. Davies, *Other Worlds*, pp. 76–77.

21. Thus, Bruce Gregory's book is entitled *Inventing Reality: Physics as Language* (New York: John Wiley, 1988); the quotation is taken from the book's jacket.

22. Bohr is quoted by Gregory in ibid., p. 196.

23. Bohm, *Quantum Theory* (Englewood Cliffs, NJ: Prentice-Hall, 1951), p. 624.

24. Davies, *The Cosmic Blueprint* (New York: Simon & Schuster, 1988), p. 168.

25. A perceptive illustration of the "collapse" of the wave function is given by Davies in *Other Worlds*, pp. 71–73.

26. John Gribbin, *In Search of Schrodinger's Cat* (New York: Bantam Books, 1984), p. 121.

27. Richard P. Feynman, *QED (Quantum Electrodynamics): The Strange Theory of Light and Matter* (Princeton, NJ: Princeton University Press, 1985), p. 5.

28. Ibid., pp. 5–6.

29. See John Hicks, *Value and Capital* (Oxford: Oxford University Press, 1939); Paul A. Samuelson, *Foundations of Economics Analysis* (Cambridge, MA: Harvard University Press, 1958); Don Patinkin, *Money, Interest, and Prices* (New York: Harper & Row, 1965); and generally, Ching-Yao Hsieh and Stephen L. Mangum, *A Search for Synthesis in Economic Theory* (Armonk, NY: M.E. Sharpe, 1986), chap. 5.

30. See Hsieh and Mangum, ibid., chap. 8.

31. Richard P. Feynman, *The Character of Physical Law* (Cambridge, MA: MIT Press, 15th ptg., 1989), p. 150.

32. Davies, *Superforce*, p. 25.

33. See ibid., chaps. 5 and 6.

34. See Hermann Weyl, *Philosophy of Mathematics and Natural Science*, p. 171; quoted in Fritjof Capra, *The Tao of Physics* (New York: Bantam Books, 1976), p. 199.

35. Davies, *Superforce*, pp. 104–7.

36. Ibid., p. 105.

37. Ibid., p. 94.

38. Richard P. Feynman, *The Character of Physical Law*, p. 103.

39. Davies, *Other Worlds*, pp. 30–31.

40. Kenneth E. Boulding, "Economics as a Moral Science," p. 120.

41. Ibid., p. 121.

42. Ibid.

43. Ibid., p. 122.

44. See Fritjof Capra's conversations with Schumacher and Henderson in *Uncommon Wisdom: Conversations with Remarkable People* (New York: Simon & Schuster, 1988).

45. From Henderson, *Creating Alternative Futures*, quoted in ibid., p. 232.

46. Paul Davidson, *Money and the Real World* (New York: John Wiley, 1972), chap. 6.

47. Paul Davidson, "Rational Expectations: A Fallacious Foundation for Studying Crucial Decision-Making Processes," *Journal of Post Keynesian Economics* 5, 2 (Winter 1982–83): 182–98. Also see in the same issue, James R. Wible, "Rational Expectations Tautologies," pp. 199–203.

48. Some representative works in this category are John D. Hey, *Economics in Disequilibrium* (New York: New York University Press, 1981), and *Uncertainty in Microeconomics* (New York: New York University Press,

1979); Franklin M. Fisher, *Disequilibrium Foundations of Equilibrium Economics* (New York: Cambridge University Press, 1983); Jean-Pascal Benessay, *The Economics of Market Disequilibrium* (New York: Academic Press, 1982); and Douglas Gale, *Money: In Disequilibrium* (Cambridge: Cambridge University Press, 1983).

49. Dugald Murdoch, *Niels Bohr's Philosophy of Physics* (Cambridge: Cambridge University Press, 1987).

50. Ibid., p. 207.

51. Ibid., p. 208.

52. Ibid., p. 243.

53. Davies, *Other Worlds*, p. 107.

54. Davies, *The Cosmic Blueprint*, p. 169.

55. Ibid., p. 170.

56. Bohm, *Wholeness and the Implicate Order*, p. 176.

57. Ibid., p. 177.

58. Ibid.

59. David Bohm, *Unfolding Meaning: A Weekend of Dialogue with David Bohm* (London: Ark Paperbacks, 1987), p. 12.

60. See *The Philosophical Writings of Niels Bohr*, vol. 3, p. 15.

61. Capra, *Uncommon Wisdom*, p. 33.

62. See the Foreword by Alan Toffler in Prigogine and Stengers, *Order out of Chaos.*

63. Erich Jantsch, *The Self-Organizing Universe* (Oxford: 1980).

64. Capra, *Uncommon Wisdom*, p. 85.

Chapter 6

Chaos Theory, Philosophy, and Economics

Contemporary physics has redirected most of its research attention to high-energy particles. This focus puts the frontier of research in physics beyond the realm of comprehension for most people. High-energy particles cannot be seen with the human eye and have no direct connection to daily life. Meanwhile, many simple things that we can observe cannot be statistically explained. For instance, such phenomena as the turbulence of fluids, the fluctuating intensity of lasers, some chemical reactions, and cardiac rhythms and arrhythmias, are only poorly understood; or simple figures we see with our naked eyes in day-to-day life, such as the shapes of clouds, or mountains, or coast lines, are never seriously measured and studied. To avoid facing these awkward and difficult tasks, scientists think of them as irregularities full of randomness and assert that few meaningful results can be learned from them.

The advance of fractal geometry and chaos theory has paved the way for physics to return to the human scale without embarrassment. Once again, physics is becoming the center of scientific development.

Chaos theory deals with objects fundamentally different from those dealt with by relativity and quantum mechanics. Nevertheless, the three theories share the same spirit in questioning the traditional view of reality. It is, thus, appropriate for us to begin this chapter with the fall of Laplacian determinism.

From Laplacian Determinism to Fundamental Uncertainty

The 18th-century French mathematician Pierre Simon de Laplace once boasted that given the current position and velocity of any particle in the universe, he could predict that particle's future for the rest of time. For more than a hundred years, most scientists shared Laplace's determinism, at least in principle. If there are any reasons that make this deterministic prediction impossible, they are rather technical ones and will be overcome sooner or later such that better and better predictions can be expected.

The first development in physical theory that proved the falsity of Laplacian determinism was Heisenberg's uncertainty principle, which states that there is a fundamental limitation to the accuracy with which the position and velocity or momentum of a particle can be measured simultaneously.[1] It seems, however, that Laplacian determinism survived the attack of the Heisenberg uncertainty principle. One might argue, without any real justification, that Laplace's assertion is in the human scale or in the macroscopic world while the Heisenberg uncertainty principle is aimed at microscopic objects.

Chaos theory occurred after Heisenberg's uncertainty principle and directly disproves Laplace's determinism. One of the pioneers of chaos theory, the French mathematician Henri Poincare, found that unpredictable "fortuitous" phenomena may occur in systems where a small change in the present causes a much larger "amplified" change in the future. In 1903 he pointed out that:

> [e]ven if it were the case that the natural laws had no longer any secret for us, we could still only know the initial situation *approximately*. If that enabled us to predict the succeeding situation with the *same approximation*, that is all we require, and we should say that the phenomenon had been predicted, that it is governed by laws. But

it is not always so: it may happen that small differences in the initial conditions produce very great ones in the final phenomenon. A small error in the former will produce an enormous error in the latter. Prediction becomes impossible, and we have the fortuitous phenomenon.[2]

The first concrete example of a chaotic system that refuted and destroyed Laplace's determinism in support of Poincare's assertion was found by Edward N. Lorenz at the Massachusetts Institute of Technology in 1963. Lorenz, a meteorologist, used a computer to simulate a simple model designed to help understand the predictability of weather. He observed that negligible perturbations are amplified to greatly affect macroscopic behavior. Two orbits with nearby initial conditions diverge exponentially fast and stay together for only a short time. Thus, long-term predictions become impossible.

As we entered the 1970s, scientists from various disciplines found similar chaotic systems, all of which led to similar conclusions of unpredictability. Among the scientists involved in these developments are Michael Henon (a French astronomer), Robert May (an Australian biologist), David Ruelle (a Belgian physicist), along with a group of American physicists such as Robert Shaw, Stephen Smale, and Mitchell Fiegenbaum, as well as such outstanding modern mathematicians as Benoit Mandelbrot, Duyne Farmer, Floris Takens, and others.

In the 1980s chaos theory bloomed. With the help of high-speed computers, calculations and graphs that were unthinkable fifty years ago can now be carried out to scrutinize the behavior of chaotic systems.

To illustrate a chaotic system, we will briefly present two examples, one mathematical and one physical. First, let us consider a system described by a simple logistic function:

$$X_{t+1} = \mu x_t (1 - x_t).$$

This deterministic iteration process can be illustrated graphically by drawing the quadratic mapping and introducing a 45-degree line, shown in Figure 6.1.

Figure 6.1. **A logistic system**

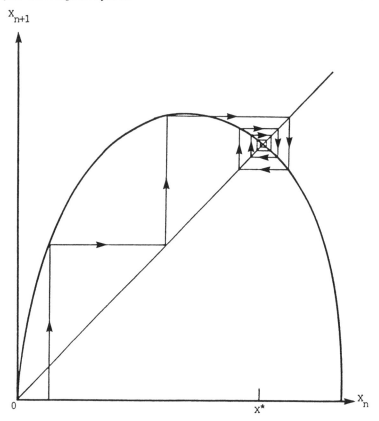

The path of the state variable of the system, x_t, can thus be derived from a given value of the parameter μ. For a small value of μ, x_t will approach either the fixed point x^*, or some limit cycles. However, for a large value of μ, say $\mu > 4$, this simple deterministic model will generate the random-looking path of x_t shown in Figure 6.2.

At least two significant implications are derived from Figure 6.2. First, an observed irregular times series of a state variable may not be essentially random, in contrast to what many scientists have believed for centuries; its underlying governing rule may be a simple deterministic, yet nonlinear, one. Second, the

Figure 6.2. **A random-looking path generated by a logistic function**

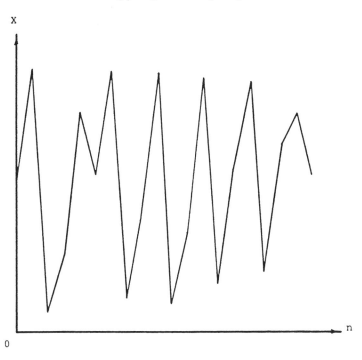

unpredictability of a chaotic system can be seen clearly from this example. A specific path, for a given μ, is determined by the initial value x_0. When μ is small, the effect of a perturbation (or a measurement error) on x_0 will vanish, or at least stay in a tolerable range as $t \to \infty$. However, when μ is large and the system becomes chaotic, a negligible measurement error in x_0 will be amplified exponentially such that any long-term prediction is absolutely impossible.

Next, let us take an example from our daily lives. If we observe a dripping faucet, we find that the time between successive drips is quite regular when the flow rate is small. As the flow rate increases, however, drops fall in a never-repeating pattern.

Letting the time interval between successive drops be the state variable, denoted x_t (using a simple microphone device, shown in

Figure 6.3. **A path generated by a dripping faucet**

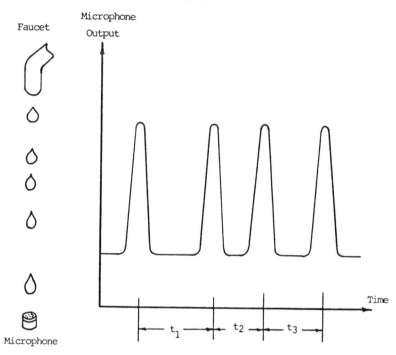

Figure 6.3, to record the x_t), we find that the path of x_t behaves similarly to the path given by the logistic iterative function. That is, x_t approaches to a fixed constant or some limit cycles when the flow rate is low, but the path becomes or looks random and unpredictable as the flow rate increases.

There is very little reason to believe that the irregular feature of the path of x_t is driven by some random factor. Actually, scientists have been convinced that in this case, the random-looking path occurs because the system is governed by an under-lying nonlinear relationship that generates complex chaotic behavior as the flow rate increases.

Although predictability is eliminated from a chaotic system, there are still things that can be learned from such a system. The most important property of a chaotic system is that the state variable will eventually settle down to a finite set, i.e., the so-called strange attractor. That is what people often said about the order in chaos. In the next section, we will further illustrate that these artistically beautifully shaped attractors are actually fractals.

Generally, we believe that there are three fundamental sources of unpredictability in reality. First, it is impossible to find the true relationship between variables. Second, it is impossible to include all relevant variables. Finally, it is impossible to measure any variable with absolute accuracy. The crucial difference between the first two sources and the last one is that the former two can be improved with improved information while the latter cannot if the underlying system is chaotic. That is why we claim that Laplace's deterministic predictability is essentially false when the system is chaotic, even when there is absolutely no random factor involved.

Fractals, and Fractals and Chaos

It should come as no surprise that when modern physics and mathematics brought the downfall of Laplace's determinism, Galileo's straight line was seriously challenged and proclaimed obsolete in many areas. To see this point, let us first read what Galileo Galilei had to say in 1623:

> [Science] is written in the language of mathematics and its characters are triangles, circles, and other geometric figures, without which it is humanly impossible to understand a single word of it; without these, one is wandering about in a dark labyrinth.[3]

It is true that these triangles, circles, and straight lines have shaped classical science and allowed it to flourish for centuries. However, the real world in which we live contains few such straight lines and perfect circles. The mountains, coastlines, cloud formations, flickering fires, and just about everything we see in nature all have complex shapes and do not consist of simple straight lines and circles.

A crusade against the straight line was championed by Frie-
densreich Hundertwasser in the 1950s:

> the straight line leads to the downfall of mankind. But the straight
> line has become an absolute tyranny. The straight line is something
> cowardly drawn with a rule, without thought and feeling; it is the
> line which does not exist in nature. And that line is the rotten founda-
> tion of our doomed civilization.[4]

More serious thought and study were finally made by the
French mathematician, Benoit Mandelbrot, who reflected:

> Clouds are not spheres, mountains are not cones, coastlines are not
> circles, and bark is not smooth, nor does lightning travel in straight
> lines. . . . Nature exhibits not in simply a higher degree but an
> altogether different level of complexity. The number of distinct
> scales of length of patterns is for all purposes infinite.
>
>   The existence of these patterns challenges us to study those forms
> that Euclid leaves aside as being formless to investigate the morphol-
> ogy of the amorphous. Mathematicians have disdained this chal-
> lenge, however, and have increasingly chosen to flee from nature by
> devising theories unrelated to anything we can see or feel.[5]

To describe the geometrical properties of mathematical objects
in nature that we *can* see and feel, Mandelbrot developed fractal
geometry.[6] The word "fractal," invented by Mandelbrot, comes
from the Latin word *fractus*, which captures the meanings of both
fraction and fracture. We will first present a fractal figure and
then illustrate fractal with an example, from the mathematical
abstract to our daily observations.

Contrary to classical geometry, which studies all regular
shapes, fractal geometry tackles irregular shapes in nature. Two
of its important features are that it simultaneously exhibits complex irregularity and yet is self-similar. Self-similarity means that
one sees similar patterns on different scales. Self-similarity can
be viewed as a symmetry across scale, in contrast to the symmetries of right to left or of top to bottom in ordinary nonfractal

Figure 6.4. **Koch curve**

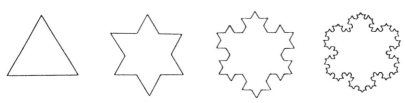

geometry. This self-similar symmetry feature goes to infinity as the scale gets finer and finer.

To get a better understanding of exactly what a fractal is, let us look at the famous Koch curve, sometimes also called the Koch snowflake, shown in Figure 6.4. It is constructed in the following way: start with a triangle with sides of length one; then, at the middle of each side, add a new triangle with sides of length $\frac{1}{3}$; and so on, into infinity. Notice that the area covered by the Koch curve is finite but the length of the curve is infinite.

The Koch curve can be used as a rough model of a coastline, if one observes, in the following way, that a coastline is in fact a fractal. Consider taking a yardstick and measuring the length of a coastline by walking it along the coastline. The yardstick skips over all twists and turns smaller than one yard, and measures the coastline shorter than it actually is. Using a smaller measure, say, a one-foot ruler, only twists and turns smaller than one foot will be skipped; but those larger than one foot and smaller than one yard (thus overlooked by the yardstick) are now added to the length to be recorded. Hence, the coastline will be recorded longer and longer with rulers of smaller and smaller length. We can measure more and more detail of the coastline, each rock, each pebble, each molecule, each atom, etc. We have to conclude that the length of a coastline is actually infinite, although it surrounds a finite area.

Now that we have seen the difference between a smooth curve and a fractal curve, how should we measure the difference between them mathematically? To do this, the so-called fractional dimension is introduced. We know that the dimension for a point is zero, for a smooth line it is one, and for a smooth plane it is two, etc. For a fractal, the situation is quite different. Take for instance, the Koch curve. It is "thicker" than a smooth line but does not really fill up the whole "band." So, it is natural to imagine that its dimension is somewhere between one and two. There are different ways to define fractional dimensions. From the popular Hausdorff definition, the dimension of the Koch curve is 1.2618.

The meaning of this fraction number 1.2618 somehow differs from the meaning of an integer number of Euclidean or topological dimension. The fractional dimension number 1.2618 tells us the degree of irregularity of the Koch curve. In general, the fractal dimension gives a qualitative measure of the degree of roughness, brokenness, or irregularity of a fractal. It is defined in such a way that it is consistent with Euclidean and topological dimensions. For example, if the fractal dimension is very close to one, we will basically see a smooth line and observe hardly any irregularity.

Finally, it should come as no surprise that chaos theory and fractal geometry are closely related. As chaos theory tries to expose the complex pattern of a dynamic system over time, fractal geometry attempts to expose the complex pattern over space; and as chaos theory attempts to find the order in disorders of a dynamic system, fractal geometry tries to find the regularity in irregularities of a fractal. The two topics now merge. An attractor gives us the order in a chaotic system and a self-similar pattern gives us the regularity in an irregular fractal. Actually, an attractor is a fractal. Figure 6.5 shows the fractal feature of the Henon attractor with enlarged scales.

The impact of chaos on the natural and social sciences may be summarized as follows: First, an integration of different scientific disciplines has been started. Science has undergone a process of specialization in the past centuries, but in the last several decades this specialization has taken a turn to generate a vast number of interdisciplines, such as biophysics, physical chemistry, mathematical economics, and so on. The emergence of these

Figure 6.5. **The Henon attractor**

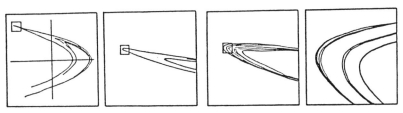

interdisciplines can be viewed as a sign of the crisis of specialization of science. Now a grand reunion of all disciplines under
the flag of chaos theory is finally taking place.

Second, through the development of chaos theory, scientists
have realized that there is a fundamental limitation regarding
human knowledge of the universe around us, especially as this
knowledge relates to predicting what is going to happen based on
what has happened. Several issues are involved. The first issue is
whether a system is intrinsically deterministic or stochastic when
a fluctuating time series of a state variable is observed from a
dynamic system. The next issue is then whether it is linear or
nonlinear if the system is indeed deterministic. If it is nonlinear,
one would want to know whether or not it is sensitive to the
initial value. These questions are asked because one needs to
determine whether an inevitable measuring error of the initial
value will converge, stay in the same range, or diverge. For the
last case, when an error is amplified, one has to conclude that
the long-term prediction becomes impossible.

There is, however, order in chaos, and patterns in irregular
fractal pictures. Even more profoundly, Crutchfield and his associates point out, ''the determinism inherent in chaos implies that
many random phenomena are more predictable than had been
thought.''[7] What we have lost, according to chaos theory, is only
the naive and primitive predictability. What we will gain from
chaos theory is some kind of more sophisticated ''predictability''
at a higher level.

Third, the development of chaos theory and fractal geometry

has dealt reductionism another debilitating blow. Let us borrow again from Crutchfield et al.:

> Chaos brings a new challenge to the reductionist view that a system can be understood by breaking it down and studying each piece. This review has been prevalent in science in the past because there are so many systems for which the behavior of the whole is indeed the sum of its parts. Chaos demonstrates, however, that a system can have complicated behavior that emerges as a consequence of simple, non-linear interaction of only a few components.[8]

Gleick's statement is even stronger:

> More and more [scientists] felt the futility of studying parts in isolation from the whole. For them, chaos was the end of the reductionist program in science.[9]

A simple dynamic system, such as the logistic one we presented in the first section of this chapter, contains only a single variable, which generates quite complicated behavior. For a chaotic system with two or three variables, such as Henon mapping or Lorenz mapping, any type of separation of the variables is literally impossible. Furthermore, as we have seen, the strange attractor of a chaotic system is a fractal, which by nature of its self-similarity across scale is impossible to break down into pieces and therefore has to studied as a whole.

Finally, the development of chaos theory is invoking new scientific methodology. Many old methods will not work for chaotic systems. New methods with new measures and new concepts are yet to come and we have sufficient reason to be optimistic when waiting for the flowering of new scientific methods as we are surrounded by all sorts of high-speed computers and hi-tech equipment.

Chaos and Philosophy

After reviewing relativity and quantum theories, in 1942 Sir James Jeans wrote: "If we must state a conclusion, it would be that many of the former conclusions of nineteenth-century science on philosophical questions are once again in the melting-pot."[10]

Recent works on the theory of chaos give additional impetus for reconsideration of the following time-honored philosophical questions: (a) being and becoming; (b) chance and necessity, or free will and determinism; (c) order and disorder; (d) mind and matter; (e) time and reality; and (f) doctrinal clashes between physics and biology.

Classical physics treated the universe as a clockwork mechanism. Time was considered a mere parameter. In the words of Paul Davies, "in classical physics there is no real change or evolution, only the rearrangement of particles."[11] The atemporal view of classical physics was also manifested in the fundamental principle of classical dynamics as reformulated by William Rowen Hamilton (see the discussion of the Hamiltonian equation in chapter 1). Furthermore, classical physics paid little attention to disorder, random processes, and fluctuations. Such aberrations from order and determinism were treated as exceptions. Hence classical physics could not provide a satisfactory answer to the ontological question of being and becoming. Nor could it throw light on the other philosophical questions mentioned above.

The irreversible arrow of time was introduced by the entropy law of thermodynamics and biology. The former described the world as evolving from order to disorder; the latter asserts that complexities in structure and organization could emerge from simple forms. Doctrinal clashes between the two scientific branches remain unresolved. The thorny question was not answered by the theory of relativity. It was simply not in the purview of Einstein at that time. Prigogine and Stengers observe: "For most of the founders of classical science—even for Einstein—science was an attempt to go beyond the world of appearances, to reach a timeless world of supreme rationality—the world of Spinoza. But perhaps there is a more subtle form of reality that involves both laws and games, time and eternity."[12] (See also Betrand Russell's quote on page 72.)

The role and meaning of time was not clearly elucidated in quantum mechanics either. For instance, once the wave function at time zero is known, its value for both the future and the past is determined. It is at this juncture that chaos enters the arena. As Paul Davies points out, "the recent works on chaos provide a bridge between chance and necessity."[13] Researchers in this area have found that dynamical systems generally have regimes of chaotic behavior and that the behavior of chaotic systems is not intrinsically indeterminate. They also begin to see that the universe is in some sense open; again, we quote Davies: "it cannot be known what new levels of variety or complexity may be in store."[14] It may be stated that chaos filled the gaps left by relativity theory and quantum mechanics. The scientific foundations have been laid for a new synthesis that would provide optimistic answers to the philosophical questions mentioned at the beginning of this discussion.

The emerging new synthesis begins with a new view of evolution. In the words of Karl Popper and John Eccles:

> Today some of us have learnt to use the word "evolution" differently. For we think that evolution—the evolution of the universe, and especially the evolution of life on earth—has produced new things. . . . The story of evolution suggests that the universe has never ceased to be creative, or "intensive."[15]

The emerging new paradigm of evolution has been explained by Erich Jantsch as follows:

> It becomes possible to view evolution as a complex, but holistic dynamic phenomenon of an universal unfolding or order which becomes manifest in many ways, as matter and energy, information and complexity, consciousness and self-reflexion. It is no longer necessary to assume a special life force (such as Bergson's elan vital or prana of hinduism) separate from the physical forces.[16]

In the emerging new paradigm, "being" and "becoming," "mind" and "matter," "order" and "disorder," "reversible time" and "irreversible time" are not irreconcilable opposites. Rather, they are complementary. "Natural history may also be understood as the evolution of consciousness or evolution of the mind."[17] This assertion of Erich Jantsch is in many ways reminiscent of the words of James Jeans: "In brief modern physics is not altogether antagonistic to an objective idealism like that of Hegel."[18]

The emerging new paradigm mentioned by Erich Jantsch is in the same vein as Ilya Prigogine and Isabelle Stengers's paradigm of self-organization. After all, Jantsch was Prigogine's most famous disciple and interpreter. At the risk of oversimplification, Prigogine and Stengers's answers to the time-honored philosophical questions stated at the beginning of this section may be outlined as follows.

On the question of time and reality, Prigogine and Stengers emphasize that irreversible time makes its appearance only in the regimes of the chaos of dynamical systems. Under such regimes of randomness, the difference between past and future would be highlighted, and irreversibility replaces reversibility of time under equilibrium conditions. Since "closed systems" may coexist with an "open universe," "reversibility" and "irreversibility" of time could be complementary. For humans, reality is embedded in the irreversible arrow of time. Thus, the two writers provide a new answer to the philosophical question of time and reality. It should be noted that the researches of the two scientists have undermined the hegemony of classical dynamics also.

On the question of chance and necessity, Prigogine and Stengers's idea of dissipative structure avoids the traditional controversies. As we stated in chapter 5, all dynamical systems contain subsystems that are continually fluctuating. The order and organization of the existing system will be shattered when the fluctuations become too powerful. The critical point reached is called a "bifurcation point." It is impossible to determine in advance which direction change will take. Here chance will push the fluctuating system down a new path. Once a new path from many other possible paths is chosen, determinism (necessity) takes over again until the next bifurcation point is reached. Thus, this new paradigm embraces both chance and necessity.

The mutualistic and nonexclusive view of Prigogine and Stengers (as well as that of Jantsch) makes it possible for physics and biology to coexist. They revised the conventional views of the second law of thermodynamics. They have shown that under nonequilibrium conditions, entropy could become the progenitor of new order and organization. Here, they rely on the "living vacuum" theory of quantum mechanics (see chapter 5), in which matter (particles) is no longer the passive substance described in classical physics. Their new view of matter is associated with the spontaneity of activity of creation. The new "active matter" enabled them to speak about a "new dialogue of man with nature."

The self-organization dynamics of Prigogine-Stengers-Jantsch also overcomes a Cartesian mind/matter duality. In the words of Erich Jantsch:

> Mind appears now as self-organizing dynamics at many levels, as a dynamics which itself evolves. In this respect, all natural history is also a history of mind. The evolutionary process does not unfold in a vacuum, but becomes manifest in the self-organization of material, energetic and informational process.[19]

This new broad concept of mind is rather similar to that of Gregory Bateson (1904–80). According to Bateson, mind manifests not only in individual organisms (including humans, of course), but also in social and ecosystems. There are deep interrelationships between mind and nature. (We may remind the reader of Bateson's words, quoted earlier: "Mind is the essence of being alive.") Bateson's unique synthesis of mind and matter evidently is in agreement with that of Prigogine-Stengers-Jantsch.

The emerging new unifying paradigm of self-organization has stressed the connections among reversible and irreversible time, order and disorder, chance and necessity, physics and biology, mind and matter. In doing so, it also enlightens us about the ontological question of being and becoming. The answer lies in the self-organization dynamics. We may also add that general relativity theory, quantum mechanics, theory of chaos, thermodynamics, and biology provided the scientific foundation of the new synthesis and that the emerging paradigm may be viewed as another illustration of the main thesis of this book.

Chaos and Economics

Chaos is the theory of complex dynamics of the mechanics that yields a time path beyond the standard tests of randomness. The roots of economists' interest in such complex dynamics, as William J. Baumol and Jess Benhabib point out, are to be found in the analysis of business cycles of the 1930s.[20] The representative works mentioned by Baumol and Benhabib are Ragnar Frisch's essay, "Propagation Problems and Impulse Problems in Dynamic Economics" (1933); Erik Lundberk's book, *Studies in the Theory of Economic Expansion* (1937); and Paul A. Samuelson's model, "Interactions between the Multiplier Analysis and the Principles of Acceleration" (1939). Among the three works, Samuelson's linear model is the most famous, having been quoted and explained in many contemporary textbooks on macroeconomics. However, according to Baumol and Benhabib, the range of possible time-path configurations generated by the linear model "simply was not sufficiently rich for the economists' purposes, since in reality time paths are often more complicated and many oscillations do not seem either to explode or dampen toward disappearance."[21]

Subsequently, in the 1950s, John Hicks and R.M. Goodwin introduced a nonlinear element in the multiplier-accelerator interaction.[22] But, say Baumol and Benhabib, "the work stopped short of introducing explicitly a degree of nonlinearity sufficiently great to generate chaotic behavior."[23]

Among the economists who have become more conscious of chaos theory in the last ten years is Jean-Michel Grandmont, who in his seminal paper applying chaos theory to economics admits:

> The techniques employed to study the occurrence and the stability of
> such business cycles are borrowed partly from recent mathematical

theories that have been constructed by using the notion of the "bifurcation" of a dynamical system in order to explain the emergence of cycles and the transition to turbulent ("chaos") behavior in physics, biological, or ecological systems.[24]

William A. Brock is another economist who pays attention to the developments in disciplines other than economics:

> Recently there has been a lot of interest in nonlinear deterministic economic models that generate highly irregular trajectories. . . . Intense exploration of low dimensional deterministic dynamical systems models has been going on in physics, chemistry, ecology, and biology, climatology and so on.[25]

One should remember that Mandelbrot himself was once considered an economist and found the fractal nature in price movement. First, he emphasized the discontinuity of price movement in order to abandon the Brownian motion model.[26] Then he proposed his scaling principle in economics to capture the self-similarity nature of a fractal observed in price movements:

> When $x(t)$ is a price, $\log x(t)$ has the property that its increment over an arbitrary time lag d, $\log x(t + d) - \log x(t)$, has a distribution independent of d, except for a scale factor.[27]

Although chaos theory has been applied to a variety of economic topics such as duopolist behavior, competitive growth, and natural resources,[28] the focal subject studied by many economists is the irregular but nevertheless recurrent pattern of GNP fluctuations over time. The issue concerning the essence of the business cycle has been sharply raised by Grandmont and Malgrange.[29] In his seminal paper, Grandmont himself, using an overlapping generations model, developed an example "in which persistent deterministic business cycles appear in a purely endogenous fashion under laissez-faire. These cycles are not attributable to exogenous 'shocks' nor to any variations of policy since there are none in the model."[30]

Since the publication of Grandmont's work, quite a few economists have been attempting to "test" for the existence of chaos in observed times series of economic variables, especially gross national product. Brock and Sayer, among others, wanted to know empirically if "the business cycle [is] characterized by deterministic chaos?" Unfortunately, their results, like others, have found weak evidence of chaos in the U.S. GNP, and they have had to conclude that "major extensions must be done before we can have confidence that this kind of work has lasting value for economic science."[31]

Grandmont also realized the limitation of his theoretical work:

> The model . . . is obviously too rudimentary to enable us to draw very general conclusions. Yet, the study of this particular example is suggestive and shows that it is possible to construct plausible models in which endogenous and significant fluctuations obtain that are not caused by exogenous shocks nor by policy.[32]

With chaos theory still in its infancy, we have no reason to be pessimistic about its future. Rather, we agree with the optimism expressed by Guy Routh who believes that chaos presents a challenge and opportunity to economists, and tells us that: "By participating, we no longer distance ourselves from the hard sciences nor from the material that forms the subject matter of reality. Instead of seeking an equilibrium that does not exist, the prime role of researchers will be to identify chaos, stress, and tension."[33]

Notes

1. See chapter 5 for a discussion of the significance of the Heisenberg uncertainty principle.

2. Quoted by J.P. Crutchfield, J.D. Farmer, N.H. Packard, and R.S. Shaw in "Chaos," *Scientific American*, December 1986, p. 48.

3. Quoted by H.O. Peitgen and P.H. Richter in *The Beauty of Fractals* (Berlin: Springer-Verlag, 1986), p. v.

4. Quoted in ibid.

5. B.B. Mandelbrot, *The Fractal Geometry of Nature* (San Francisco: W.H. Freeman, 1982), p. 1.

6. Ibid.

7. Crutchfield et al., "Chaos," p. 56.

8. Ibid., p. 56.

9. James Gleick, *Chaos: Making a New Science* (New York: Viking 1987), p. 304.

10. Sir James Jeans, *Physics and Philosophy* (Ann Arbor: University of Michigan Press, 1966), p. 216.

11. Paul Davies, *The Cosmic Blueprint* (New York: Simon & Schuster, 1988), p. 197.

12. Ilya Prigogine and Isabelle Stengers, *Order out of Chaos* (New York: Bantam Books, 1984), p. 310.

13. Davies, *The Cosmic Blueprint*, p. 52.

14. Ibid., p. 56.

15. Karl Popper and John Eccles, *The Self and its Brain* (Berlin: Springer International, 1977), p. 61.

16. Erich Jantsch, *The Self-Organizing Universe* (Oxford: Pergamon Press, 1980), p. 307.

17. Ibid.

18. Sir James Jeans, *Physics and Philosophy*, p. 204.

19. Erich Jantsch, *The Self-Organizing Universe*, p. 307.

20. William J. Baumol and Jess Benhabib, "Chaos: Significance, Mechanism, Economic Applications," *Journal of Economic Perspectives 3*, 1 (Winter 1989):77–105.

21. Ibid., p. 79.

22. See John Hicks, *A Contribution to the Theory of the Trade Cycle* (New York: Oxford University Press, 1950); and R.M. Goodwin, "The Non-linear Accelerator and the Persistence of Business Cycles," *Econometrica 19* (1951).

23. Baumol and Benhabib, "Chaos," p. 79.

24. J. Grandmont, "On Endogenous Competitive Business Cycles," *Econometrica 53* (1985):995.

25. W.A. Brock, "Distinguishing Random and Deterministic Systems: Abridged Version," *Journal of Economic Theory 40* (1986):168.

26. See Mandelbrot, *The Fractal Geometry of Nature*, p. 335.

27. Mandelbrot, "The Variation of Certain Speculative Prices," *Journal of Business 36* (1963):394–419.

28. Many of these papers can be found in the *Journal of Economic Theory 40* (1986).

29. See J. Grandmont and P. Malgrange, "Nonlinear Economic Dynamics: Introduction," *Journal of Economic Theory 40* (1986):3–12.

30. J. Grandmont, "On Endogenous Competitive Business Cycles," pp. 995–1045.

31. W.A. Brock and C.L. Sayers: "Is the Business Cycle Characterized by Deterministic Chaos?" *Journal of Monetary Economics 22* (1988):77–90.

32. Grandmont, "On Endogenous Competitive Business Cycles," pp. 995–1045.

33. See Guy Routh, "Economics and Chaos," *Challenge* (July-August 1989), p. 51.

Chapter 7

The Revolutions in Physics and the Future of Economics

What will be the impact of relativity, quantum theory, and chaos theory on the future of economics? Being of average mind, we do not pretend to know the answer. In searching for some clue that will shed light on the difficult question, we keep in mind, first of all, the following observation of Mark Blaug:

> The so-called Copernican revolution . . . took a hundred and fifty years to complete and was argued out every step of the way; even the Newtonian revolution took more than a generation to win acceptance through the scientific circles of Europe, during which time the Cartesians, Leibnizians, and Newtonians engaged in bitter disputes over every aspect of the new theory; likewise in the twentieth century classical to relativistic and quantum physics involved . . . [a great deal of controversies.].[1]

Second, in attempting to brush away the cobwebs in our minds, we set the question in the context of some leading reconstructions of economics suggested since the conquest of the mechanistic world view. At the risk of oversimplification, we have grouped the suggested reconstructions under two categories:

I. *Suggested Methodological Revisions without "Paradigm Shifts"*
   1. The Popper-Blaug critique
   2. Dissensions of the Modern Austrian School
   3. Arrow-Hahn and Franklin M. Fisher's price-adjustment processes
   4. Other nontatonnement microeconomic models
   5. Rational expectations
II. *Arguments for Revolutionary "Paradigm Shifts"*
   1. The German Historical School of economics
   2. Marxism
   3. Institutionalism
   4. Modern antigrowth theories
   5. Holism inspired by relativity, quantum theory, and chaos theory

The central idea of the Blaug-Popper critique has been explained by Mark Blaug:

> Like many other modern economists, I too have a view of *What's Wrong With Economics?* to cite the title of a book by Benjamin Ward, but my quarrel is less with the actual content of modern economics than with the way economists go about validating their theories. I hold that there is nothing much wrong with standard economic methodology . . . ; what is wrong is that economists do not practice what they preach.[2]

In other words, Robert S. Goldfarb writes:

> While according to Blaug the majority of [the] economic profession seems to believe conceptually in the appropriateness of [Popperian] falsificationism, "the problem now is to persuade economists to take falsificationism seriously" by actually practicing it.[3]

Falsificationism is the methodological tradition established by Karl Popper, the leading spokesman of the new view of the philosophy of science, which is largely concerned with the logical analysis of the formal structure of scientific theories. The two pillars of the old view of philosophy of science are inductionism and verifiability. The scientific foundation of inductionism is Newtonian physics; verifiability means that both the assumptions and the predictions of theories must be tested against facts. Thus, verifiability is closely linked to the philosophy of logical positivism. Popper rejects both inductionism and verifiability. Following David Hume, Popper stresses that there is a fundamental asymmetry between induction and deduction. In the philosophy of science this asymmetry is called the "problem of induction." Hume argued that one cannot provide an inductive proof to the conclusion that the sun will rise tomorrow, which is deduced from past experience. In the words of Lawrence A. Boland, "This leads many of us to ask 'So how do we know that the sun will rise tomorrow?' If it is impossible to provide a proof, then presumably we would have to admit that we do not know!"[4]

In rejecting the "verifiability methodology" of the logical positivists, Popper introduced the new methodology of falsification which regards theories and hypotheses as scientific if, and only if, their predictions are empirically falsifiable. Mark Blaug cites a favorite Popperian example of falsificationism: "No amount of observations of white swans can allow the inference that all swans are white, but the observation of a single black swan is enough to refute that conclusion."[5]

There were substantial overlaps between modern Austrian subjective economics and neoclassical orthodoxy as observed by Gerald P. O'Driscoll, Jr., and Mario J. Rizzo.[6] However, the modern Austrian subjective economics goes beyond the subjective utility theory of neoclassical orthodoxy. Israel M. Kirzner stresses that there are two distinct insights of the Austrian school that are different from neoclassical orthodoxy:

> First, there is the insight that human action is purposeful, and second, there is the insight that there is indeterminacy and unpredictability inherent in human preference, human expectations and human knowledge.[7]

The common thread tying together the various Austrian doctrines is the notion of historical (real) time which has been abstracted from neoclassical orthodoxy.[8] The modern Austrian economists argue that utility maximization depends on the individual's imagination and alertness to new opportunities and that the seizing of opportunities requires knowledge and expectations. Both knowledge and expectations formation are inseparable from historical time. In historical time, the future is uncertain. Without perfect foresight, individuals make mistakes. Expectations frequently are unfulfilled. This is the source of disequilibrium. In a world of disequilibrium, individuals learn to avoid mistakes. Thus, their purposeful actions (praxeology) become more and more coordinated. A movement to restore equilibrium is thus initiated.

Although the Austrian economists shared the same cultural roots as Popper and the philosophers of logical positivism, they believe that the axioms of praxeology are valid a priori, that is, that they are not subject to verification or falsification on the ground of experiences and facts.

Two other distinguishing features of the school should be noted:

1. Refection of "scientism in the study of man": Murray N. Rothbard asserts that "Scientism is the profound unscientific attempt to transfer uncritically the methodology of the physical sciences to the study of human action."[9] F.A. Hayek shared this view.[10]

2. Preference of the short-run view: Lawrence A. Boland writes:

> Economists from the Austrian School do not recommend free-enterprise capitalism because it necessarily leads to Adam Smith's world of long-run equilibrium. On the contrary, as we saw with Hayek, to the extent that reaching any long-run equilibrium requires the acquisition of correct knowledge (or the correct expectations), reaching a long-run equilibrium is never possible. Besides that, what constitutes a long-run equilibrium depends on the exogenous given, and we all know that they change faster than the process can ever get us to any long-run equilibrium.[11]

In other words, the Austrians' emphasis on historical time and its attendant uncertainty is the reason for their distrust about long-run equilibrium analysis.

On the question of historical time, there is much common ground between the tenets of the post-Keynesian school[12] and those of the modern Austrian economists. However, as O'Driscoll and Rizzo observe, "Cross-fertilization between these two schools is exceedingly rare."[13] One possible explanation for this impasse could be the Austrians' deep suspicion of macroeconomics. They frequently call post-Keynesian writers "neo-Ricardians."

The next suggested methodological revision within the paradigm of neoclassical orthodoxy is the topic of Arrow-Hahn and Fisher's price-adjustment processes. Such suggestions open the "Pandora's box" of disequilibrium foundations of general equilibrium theory, for general equilibrium theories need disequilibrium foundations and disequilibrium theory requires stability analysis.[14]

The year 1960 saw a renaissance of stability analysis. The prime movers in this new wave were F.H. Hahn, H. Uzawa, and T. Negishi.[15] The distinguishing new features of this literature are:

(a) They give more consideration to trade out-of-equilibrium and to disequilibrium behavior.

(b) Price adjustments and nontatonnement stability are attained via the Lyapounov functions. According to Franklin M. Fisher, "Such Lyapounov functions have tended to go from geometrically interpretable measures of the distance from equilibrium to economically more interesting functions such as the sum of the utilities which households would expect to get if their mutually inconsistent plans could be realized."[16]

(c) The institutional framework is a pure exchange economy without production.

As pointed out by Franklin M. Fisher, in their *General Competitive Analysis* (1971), K.J. Arrow and F.H. Hahn constructed a revised version of the "Hahn process" by introducing a money commodity. They suggested the following stability conditions:

(a) "Positive cash assumption" (a name coined by Fisher): this assumption states that no one ever runs out of money in transactions;

(b) "Present action postulate," which assumes that households must act immediately when they encounter effective excess demand;

(c) "Orderly market," which implies that there will not be any frustrated demands or supplies after trade; and

(d) The last stability condition is named by Fisher as "naive expectation of trading agents" which means that trading agents believe that the market will be in equlibrium.

In 1986 Fisher generalized the "Hahn process" by basing price adjustment on the optimal decisions of agents, instead of trusting to a *deus ex machina*, the Walrasian "auctioneer." In his stability analysis, Fisher discards the assumption of "naive expectations." The Fisherian traders are constantly aware of disequilibrium (Fisher's "disequilibrium consciousness") and are allowed to make price offers and arbitrage whenever they perceive favorable opportunities. The only restrictive stability condition required is what Fisher calls the condition of "no favorable surprise," which means that sudden optimistic revisions in agents' expectations must be ruled out. In Fisher's opinion, there is one overriding fact that is far more important than the technical details of convergence: this is the "hysteresis effect" (which we considered in chapter 1).

The fourth item in our first category is "other nontatonnement microeconomic models."[17] Since it is not our objective to make an exhaustive survey of such models, it should suffice to remind readers of a few distinguishing types of the existing ones. First, we should mention the microfoundations of post-Keynesian macroeconomics. Among the post-Keynesians there is increasing awareness of the limitations of the Sraffian and other neo-Ricardian arguments about the set of "normal [natural] prices" which must prevail in the long run if the system is to be capable of maintaining steady-state growth. In the view of Alfred S. Eichner, "Post-Keynesians should formulate disequilibrium models with a view to providing a more viable microfoundation of macroeconomics."[18] Following Eichner's clarion call, Nina Shapiro, Nai-Pew Ong, Josef Steindl, and others have studied changes in markup pricing over time.[19] Other nontatonnement models included in one of the author's earlier surveys are Harvey Leibenstein's X-efficiency theory of the firm, Cyert and March's behavioral theory of the firm, the theory of incomplete information, and the theory of implicit contract.

The fifth item is "rational expectations." Since most graduate students of economics are familiar with this theory, we will only highlight the mission of the rational expectations school. To the writers of this school, too many irrational elements and inconsistencies of Keynesian economics are still retained in the models of the "neoclassical synthesis."[20] Thus, the school's main objective is to apply neoclassical utility optimization principles to all economic problems, specifically to the problems of expectations formation and macroeconomic policy. While many criticisms can be leveled at the rational expectations hypothesis, one should not obscure its accomplishments. In the words of Rodney Maddock and Michael Carter, "it brings to the fore questions about the availability and use of information. Instead of being the finale of the monetarist's case against policy intervention, it should be seen as the prologue for a revitalized theory of expectations, information and policy."[21]

We turn now to our second category—the arguments for revolutionary "paradigm shifts" in economics. The revolutions in physics have provided new impetus to the reconstruction of economics. In the history of economic thought we have witnessed several "paradigm shifts" nudged by changes in world views that were in turn nurtured by important revolutions in physics. In chapter 1 we attempted to describe the threefold relationships among Newtonian physics, the mechanistic world view, and economics. In our second chapter we considered the impact of the two laws of thermodynamics on the Cartesian-Newtonian mechanistic world view. The antigrowthmania economists of the twentieth century generally rejected reductionism and embraced instead a holistic approach to economic problems.

In chapter 2 we also described the nineteenth-century "Romantic Revolt against the Mechanistic World View." The romantics embraced the organic view of nature. They inclined to reject Newtonian mechanics and champion biology instead. In this respect it may be tempting to think that the threefold relationship (the main theme of this book) is broken. However, one should keep in mind that the romantics' theory of evolution was essentially philosophical. Even August Comte, who placed biology at the top of his hierarchy of sciences, did not formulate any scientific biological theory. Comte died in 1859 before the publication of Charles Darwin's *Origin of Species* in the same year. Furthermore, the important advances in the biological sciences came after the heyday of the Romantic movement. In the twentieth century, almost all modern biologists have accepted the mechanistic paradigm. We have witnessed the rise of the so-called "mechanistic theory of life," which, in the words of Paul Davies, "maintains that living organisms are complex machines which function according to the usual laws of physics, under the action of ordinary physical forces. Differences between animate and inanimate matters are attributed to the different levels of complexity alone."[22] Thus, living cells are described as "factories" under the ultimate control of DNA molecules "which organize the 'assembly' of basic molecular 'units' into larger structures according to a 'program' encoded in the molecular machinery."[23]

Although it has been said that biology is just a branch of chemistry, which is in turn just a branch of physics, yet the evolutionary hypothesis of biology (which was not within the purview of Newtonian mechanics) did set down the basic theme of practically all the important writings of the nineteenth century, including the German Historical School of economics and the young Karl Marx's 1844 *Manuscripts* (discussed in chapter 2).

The German Historical School's suggestions for reconstruction of economics were based on the following arguments: (a) that the correct procedure for the study of economics should be historical investigation; (b) that such historical investigations would in time lead to the formulation of general laws through induction (recall the Popperian ''problem of induction'' mentioned earlier in this chapter; the asymmetry of induction and deduction may be one cause for the decline of the Historical School); and (c) that general laws of economics are historically relative because the data on which they are based would change over time. In other words, members of the school stressed that there are no universal economic laws and that there should be differences in policy conclusions according to the different sociocultural framework under investigation. In addition, they rejected the psychological foundations of classical economics as well as the abstract reasoning of the Ricardian models. In the tradition of the Romantic movement, the German Historical School argued for a holistic approach to the study of economics.

The gist of the young Marx's *Economic and Philosophical Manuscripts* has been perceptively summarized by Ivan Svitak, who said, ''Communism without humanism is no communism and humanism without communism cannot be humanism.''[24] Had Russia and China followed the argument of the young Marx, Stalinistic repressions and the terrorism of the ''Red Guards'' could have been avoided. The failure of Marxism to explain the durability of capitalism and the slow growth of the socialist economies have caused deep soul searching and disillusionment among many thinking Marxists. This sentiment is reflected in the famous quip of the French Maoist, Michel le Bris: ''God is dead; Marx is dead; and I don't feel too well myself.'' The recent democratic movements in Eastern Europe and elsewhere have shown that the aspiration of the Marxian reconstruction of economics is practically over. Long before the recent earthshaking events, Anthony Cutler, Barry Hindess, Paul Hirst, and Athar Hussain pinpointed in 1977 the major theoretical weakness of Marxian economics. They stressed that ''Marxism currently has no adequate theory of modern monetary forms, of financial capitalist institutions. . . . The theorization in *Capital* of money, credit, capitalist organization and calculation are all seriously inadequate."[25]

The Darwinian theory of evolution also had a strong influence on Thorstein Veblen's (1857–1929) arguments for the reconstruction of economics. Like the writers of the German Historical School, Veblen sought to give a genetic account of capitalism, or the enterprise system, and to set forth the motivations and institutions peculiar to this system. According to Wesley Clair Mitchell, who was Veblen's student and friend, "Darwin tells what stimulation he received from reflecting upon Malthus' theory of population when he was groping after his own theory of natural selection. An installment upon this debt of biology to economics was paid by the stimulation that Darwin's doctrines gave to Veblen's theory of cultures."[26] In *The Place of Science in Modern Civilization*, Veblen criticized Marxian dialectical materialism as pre-Darwinian:

> The assumed goal of the Marxian process of class struggle is conceived to cease in the classless economic structure of the socialistic final term. In Darwinianism there is no such final and perfect term, and no definite equilibrium.[27]

Veblen also attacked neoclassical orthodoxy as expounded by his first teacher in economics, John Bates Clark. His fundamental criticism against orthodox economists is that their conception of science is pre-Darwinian; therefore they have asked the wrong questions. Their hedonistic pleasure and pain calculus and their logic of optimal choice were treated by Veblen with contempt. In Veblen's view, economic rationality is socially and culturally determined. Hence the epistemological unit is the institution. Institutions evolve. Therefore economics should be an evolutionary science. In the words of Ben B. Seligman, "Veblen was seeking a 'holistic' approach, one in which economics would evolve into a genuinely cultural science. It was the institutionalist contention that the market was not the sole area for economic action."[28]

Veblen's institutionalism is also influenced by his teacher, Charles Pierce, who initiated the distinctive American philosophy of pragmatism. Unfortunately, as Philip Mirowski observes, Veblen "thoroughly misunderstood Pierce's hermeneutics, . . . the Achilles heel of his system was his naive conception of science and the exalted place of the engineers."[29]

What *is* Charles Pierce's hermeneutics? According to Mirowski:

> Hermeneutics concentrates on the role of shared tradition as the locus of continuity and quality control in the interpretative process; it therefore follows that the discipline of history is an indispensable accessory of hermeneutics. Hermeneutics is generally hostile to the Cartesian tradition of analytic philosophy, especially the presumption of the mind-body dichotomy and the program of mechanical reduction.[30]

The Piercian legacy was subsequently adopted by the other founding father of institutional economics, John Rogers Commons.

An institution is defined by Commons as collective action in control, liberation, and expansion of individual action. The determination of prices is not something that arises out of market only. To Commons, prices are determined by the purposeful transactions of many individuals and groups within the setting of law and custom, where the ultimate arbiter is the Supreme Court. Thus, economics, ethics, and law combine to create a system of "reasonable values." The Piercian hermeneutics is clearly reflected in Commons's views.

Unlike Veblen's theory, Commons's institutionalism is an operating theory. His pragmatism led him to ask: How do our economic institutions work, and why do they work? Commons believed that conflict of interest was inevitable in a private-property, free-enterprise economy. Unlike Marx, however, Commons stressed that these conflicts could be resolved by compromises through "collective bargaining." Undoubtedly, Commons was America's greatest labor economist in his time.

It is beyond the scope of this book to capture the whole of

institutional economics. We would like to conclude this section by quoting the following observation of Philip Mirowski:

> The project of the founding fathers of institutional economics [Veblen, Commons, and Wesley Mitchell] was to confront and disarm the mechanistic structure of economics . . . their major theme that resonates among their otherwise disparate writings was that they were all united "against mechanism." Their project faltered because it failed to take into account the actual structure and practices of physics, and because it ultimately misunderstood the dangers of trying to appropriate the legitimacy of science.[31]

The fourth item in our second category concerns modern anti-growth theories. The subject has been considered in chapter 2, to which the reader is referred.

There are many differences among the four suggested "paradigm shifts" outlined in the preceding paragraphs. Nevertheless, they have one feature in common: they all reject the mechanistic world view. Their advocacy of holism is parallel not only to classical Greek philosophy, Chinese taoism, and Indian religious thought, but also to the general drift of relativity theory, quantum mechanics, and chaos theory. In the words of Niels Bohr, "For a parallel to the lesson of atomic theory . . . [we must turn] to those kinds of epistemological problems with which already thinkers like the Buddha and Lao Tzu have been confronted, when trying to harmonize our position as spectators and actors in the great drama of existence."[32]

We turn now to the last entry in our second category, namely, "holism inspired by relativity, quantum theory, and chaos theory." As we mentioned in chapters 4 through 6, the universe as interpreted by relativity, quantum, and chaos theories is an undivided and unbroken whole. Although Einstein found it difficult to accept quantum uncertainty, yet in his search for a unified field theory he was inching toward the new direction in physics. For instance, in his General Theory, Einstein abolished the Newtonian force of gravity and introduced the revolutionary new concept of warped space-time. In one stroke he demonstrated that space and time were no longer just the absolute stage on which particles move, as hypothesized in Newtonian physics. Space-time is indeed one of the actors. Furthermore, David Bohm observes that Einstein took the total field of the whole universe as a primary description:

> This field is continuous and indivisible. Particles are then to be regarded as certain kinds of abstraction from the total field, corresponding to regions of very intense field (called singularities). . . . Thus, we come to an order that is radically different from that of Galileo and Newton—the order of undivided wholeness.[33]

The holistic quantum world has been penetratingly illustrated by Richard Feynman using the so-called two-slit experiment. Feynman wrote: "It will take just this one experiment, which has been designed to contain all of the mystery of quantum mechanics."[34] John Gribbin points out that the experiment highlights the important point that "the whole thing is what matters—the apparatus, the electrons, and the observer are all part of the experiment. . . . The world seems to keep all its options, all its probabilities. . . . [I]t is the act of observing a system that forces it to select one of its options, which then becomes real."[35] In terms of Schrodinger's wave function, this is called the "collapse of the wave function" by physicists.

The nonlinear approach of chaos reaffirms the view that the whole is greater than its parts. In Paul Davies's words, "The new paradigm amounts to turning three hundred years of entrenched philosophy on its head. To use the words of physicist Pedrag Cvitanovic, 'Junk our old equations and look for guidance in clouds' repeating patterns.' It is, in short, nothing less than a brand new start in the description of nature."[36] The impact of this new approach has prompted James Gleick to make the following report: "More and more [scientists] felt the futility of studying parts in isolation from the whole. For them, chaos was the end of the reductionist program in science."[37] The sentiment for the resurgence of holism has indeed been spreading. For instance, Fritjof Capra reports:

> Physicians in the United States, Canada, and Europe are forming associations and holding conferences to discuss the merits of holistic medicine. As a result of these discussions doctors are trying to eliminate unnecessary surgery, diagnostic tests, and prescriptions, recognizing that this will be the most effective way to bring down health costs.[38]

On the question of ecology, Capra observes, "To emphasize the deeper meaning of ecology, philosophers and scientists have begun to make a distinction between 'deep ecology' and 'shallow environmentalism.' "[39] The former recognized that ecological balance requires changes in our perception of the role of human beings in the planetary ecosystem; the latter is concerned only with more efficient control and management of the natural environment. In addition, there have been holistic movements in psychology, physiology, mathematics, and other fields.

To answer our question about the future of economics in light of the revolution in physics, it is very tempting to join the chorus of holism. "It would be a great mistake," cautions Davies, "to present reductionism and holism as somewhat locked in irreconcilable combat for our allegiance. They are really two complementary rather than conflicting paradigms. There has always been a place for both in properly conducted science."[40] One should not forget the fact, Davies tells us, that "Newton's theory remains satisfactory for all practical purposes, such as aircraft and spacecraft navigation, and is still adequate for the description of astronomical systems."[41] Fritjof Capra, who firmly advocates a strong systems approach as the solution of the various crises facing us today, also acknowledges that Cartesian reductionism "has proved extremely useful in the development of scientific theories and the realization of complex technological projects. It was Descartes' method that made it possible for NASA to put a man on the moon."[42]

If the complementarity of reductionism and holism is any guide, we may expect that economists will continue their efforts in sharpening their tools for short and intermediate-run problem solving. In so doing, we should not forget (a) Franklin M.

Fisher's warning that the "hysteresis effect" is far more important than technical details for convergence (which we discussed
earlier in this chapter as well as chapter 1), and (b) Philip
Mirowski's admonition that "economics needs protection from
itself."[43] In other words, economists should not develop some
sort of "superiority complex" or delude themselves that economics is superior to other social sciences in rigor, precision, or
technical expertise.

In the long run economists should not lose sight of the
changing perception of reality that has resulted from the second
revolution in physics. The three-hundred-year entrenched Cartesian-Newtonian world view has planted in our mind that the
world has objective characteristics that exist independently of
our observations (Descartes' *res extensa*). We have been
trained to relate to such a perception of "reality." The persistent resistance to the new physics may be traced to a large
extent to our entrenched belief in the "objective" reality. As
Bruce Gregory observes, "There is a sense in which no one,
including philosophers, doubts the existence of a real objective
world. The stubbornly physical nature of the world we encounter everyday is obvious."[44] Furthermore, this belief has been
reinforced by "pictures" provided by classical physics. Gregory also notes that "Classical physics replaced the question
why [of Aristotelian-Thomasian physics] with the question
how. In the language of Newton and Maxwell, answers to the
latter question come in the form of descriptions of motion [of
absolute particles] through [absolute] space and [absolute]
time. The new language of quantum mechanics replaces the
question *how* with the question *what*."[45]

Gregory's perceptive observation can be substantiated by the
writings of the founding fathers of quantum mechanics. Niels
Bohr said, "There is no quantum world. There is only abstract
quantum physics description. It is wrong to think that the task of
physics is to find out how nature is. Physics is concerned only
with what we can say about nature."[46] And Werner Heisenberg
warns:

we have to remember that what we observe is not nature in itself but nature exposed to our method of questioning . . . quantum theory reminds us, as Bohr has put it, of the old wisdom that when searching for harmony in life one must never forget that in the drama of existence we are ourselves both players and spectators. It is understandable that in our scientific relation to nature our own activity becomes very important when we have to deal with parts of nature into which we can penetrate only by using the most elaborate tools.[47]

The position of Bohr and Heisenberg on reality is lucidly explained by Bruce Gregory:

Quantum mechanics is a way of talking about nature that allows physicists to predict how the world will respond to being measured. So long as we stick to this understanding, quantum mechanics raises no problems. If, on the other hand, we persist in demanding to know how the world is, independent of how it appears to be in experiment, we, in Feynman's words "will get down the drain, into a blind alley from which nobody has yet escaped."[48]

Indeed, many of us are still trapped in Feynman's "blind alley," for the picture of reality based on classical Newtonian physics is very appealing. We can easily visualize myriads of elementary particles like solid balls, locked together to form a familiar object such as a rock. The whole (rock) is simply the sum of its parts (elementary particles). This classical linear relationship between the whole and its parts has been overturned by new physics. "The quantum factor," says Paul Davies, "forces us to perceive particles only in relation to the whole."[49] In other words, the universe is a network of relations, Davies writes, "an inseparable web of vibrating energy patterns in which no one component has reality independently of the entirety; and included in the entirety is the observer."[50]

This changed perception of reality provides the scientific foundation of the following arguments for reconstruction of economics:

1. Institutional economics with a Piercian hermeneutic perspective (considered earlier in this chapter).

2. The new wave of socioeconomics advocated by Amitai Etzioni, Richard Swedberg, Paul C. Stern, and others.[51]

3. Fritjof Capra's suggestion that the economics profession could adopt Geoffrey Chew's "bootstrap approach" in modeling.

According to Etzioni, modern socioeconomics seeks to correct the view of neoclassical economics that all moral rights are invested in the individual by giving the community a moral status equal to the individual:

> The more recent socioeconomic conception of individuals and communities as interdependent attempts to correct this radical individualism. . . . The implications of socioeconomics for the future of research, public policy, and education are many and varied. The new discipline can aid economic research, for example, precisely because it deals with both individual desires and moral commitments when studying human economic behavior. For instance, to understand noncompliance with tax laws, we need to know more than just the tax rates. We need to know the extent to which people consider the tax system fair or unfair.[52]

Richard Swedberg points out that the term "socioeconomics" was coined by the German economist and sociologist, Max Weber (1864–1920). The main point for Weber was that economists should draw simultaneously on conventional economic theory, history, and sociology. Swedberg writes:

> A strategy that is recommended for socioeconomics today can be centered around three propositions: (1) There should be multiple approaches to economic problems; (2) The borders between economics and other social sciences must be kept open; and (3) Allowance must be made for the complexity of human behavior and culture.[53]

Although the new socioeconomists have not mentioned the revolution in physics, yet their basic tenet that economics and other social sciences are interrelated is compatible with the perception of the new physics that the universe is a network of relations. Hence we suggest that this new perception of reality could be the scientific foundation of the new discipline.

Reality envisioned by relativity, quantum, and chaos theories is compatible with the revitalized institutionalism also. Following Dugald Murdoch, there is a pragmatist strain in Niels Bohr's thought, whereas Heisenberg's philosophy is unmistakeably positivist. In Murdoch's words, "The positivists and pragmatists share an abhorrence of speculative metaphysics, regarding as meaningless ontological questions that do not admit of a decisive answer on the basis of experience."[54] Both the revitalized institutionalism and the new physics reject the Laplacian deterministic predictability.

Geoffry Chew's bootstrap approach was designed to develop a comprehensive theory of strongly interacting particles as well as a more general philosophy of nature. "According to this bootstrap philosophy," explains Fritjof Capra, "nature cannot be reduced to fundamental building blocks of matter, but has to be understood entirely through self-consistency. . . . The universe is seen as a dynamic web of interrelated events. None of the properties of any of this web is fundamental; they all follow from the properties of the other parts, and the overall consistency of their interrelations determines the structure of the entire web."[55]

The bootstrap approach is never appropriate for any individual model, but can be applied only to a combination of mutually consistent models, none of which is any more fundamental than the others.[56] Thus, the bootstrap approach could be adopted by revitalized institutional economics, or socioeconomics, as well as by the economics profession.

On a limited scale some interdisciplinary approaches have been adopted by a number of economists. For instance, Martin Shubik predicted in 1970:

> Since the defeat of the institutionalists, there have been many new developments in economics that I believe are going to result in a joining together of detailed institutional studies, advanced mathematical theory and political economy. I expect that a new microeconomics is about to emerge. It can be described (in a ponderous manner) as mathematical-institutional-political economy.[57]

Subsequent developments in economic theory prove that Shubik's prediction is not an impossible dream. The post-Keynesians have always stressed the importance of institutional factors in both macroeconomics and microeconomics. "Post-Keynesian theory," Alfred S. Eichner writes, "is meant to describe an economic system with advanced credit and other monetary institutions—all of which play a fundamental role in the dynamic process being analyzed."[58] General equilibrium theorists such as Frank H. Hahn, Kenneth Arrow, and Franklin M. Fisher likewise have paid increasing attention to institutional developments. The non-tatonnement models mentioned earlier in this chapter also affirm Shubik's insight. "Since the 1970s," observes socioeconomist Richard Swedberg, "something has started to happen in the division of labor between economics and the other social sciences. We see, for example, economists like Gary Becker and Oliver Williamson taking on traditional sociological topics, and we see sociologists like Harrison White and Mark Granovetter taking on traditional economic topics."[59]

Unfortunately, Swedberg stresses, "During the 1980s 'economic imperialism' became increasingly accepted, both in the United States and elsewhere."[60] It is Swedberg's contention that "economic imperialism" threatens to set off a new "battle of methods," which could have very negative consequences for economics, just like the original *Methodenstreit* around the turn of the century. We hasten to add that should the impending new *Methodenstreit* be set off, counterproductive consequences could be inflicted on other social sciences too.

To make any multidisciplinary approach workable, we venture to suggest that economists and other social scientists, as well as physical scientists, should rekindle the time-honored virtues of humility and generosity. Perhaps economists should curb their aspiration of formulating the economic interpretation of human behavior. Other social scientists should learn to supplement their insights by the insights of the economists. Maybe physicists should also forget about seeking a single, Lagrangian formula to explain the entire universe simple enough to be worn on a tee-shirt. For knowledge can best flourish when it is accompanied by humility and generosity.

Notes

1. Mark Blaug, *The Methodology of Economics: Or How Economists Explain* (Cambridge: Cambridge University Press, 1980), p. 31. Also see Thomas S. Kuhn, *The Structure of Scientific Revolutions*, 2nd ed., enl. (Chicago: University of Chicago Press, 1970).

2. Blaug, *Methodology of Economics*, p. xiii.

3. Cited from an unpublished research paper by Robert S. Goldfarb entitled "If (as M. Blaug, H. Johnson, W. Leontief, B. Ward and Others Have Claimed) Economists Do Not Severely Test Their Theories, What's All This Empirical Work in Economics about, Anyway?" Goldfarb's paper considers how well the Blaug critique applies to several empirical literatures in applied economics, and also asks what other empirical tasks besides falsificationist theory testing these empirical literatures might be carrying out.

4. Lawrence A. Boland, *The Foundations of Economic Method* (London: Allen & Unwin, 1982), p. 13.

5. Mark Blaug, *Methodology of Economics*, p. 12.

6. See Ching-Yao Hsieh and Stephen L. Mangum, *A Search for Synthesis in Economic Theory* (Armonk, NY: M.E. Sharpe, 1986), p. 129.

7. Israel Kirzner, "On the Method of Austrian Economics," in Edwin G. Dolan, ed., *The Foundations of Modern Austrian Economics* (Kansas City, MO: Sheed & Ward, 1976), p. 42.

8. See Hsieh and Mangum, *A Search for Synthesis*, chap. 6, pp. 129–35.

9. See chapter 2.

10. See chapter 2.

11. Boland, *Foundations of Economic Method*, p. 169.

12. For a short guide to post-Keynesian economics, see Hsieh and Mangum, *A Search for Synthesis*, chap. 8.

13. G.P. O'Driscoll, Jr., and M.J. Rizzo, *The Economics of Time and Ignorance* (New York: Basil Blackwell, 1985), p. 9.

14. For a nontechnical consideration of Franklin M. Fisher's *Disequilibrium Foundations of Equilibrium Economics* (Cambridge: Cambridge University Press, 1983), see Hsieh and Mangum, *A Search for Synthesis*, chap. 10.

15. See Frank H. Hahn, "A Stable Adjustment Process for a Competitive Economy," *Review of Economic Studies* 29 (1962):62–65; Frank H. Hahn, "On the Stability of Pure Exchange Equilibrium," *International Economic Review* 3 (1962):206–13; Frank H. Hahn and T. Negishi, "A Theorem on Non-Tatonnement Stability," *Econometrica* 30 (1962):179–86; H. Uzawa, "The Stability of Dynamic Process," *Econometrica* 29 (1961):317–31; and H. Uzawa, "On the Stability of Edgeworth's Barter Process," *International Economic Review 3* (1962):218–82.

16. For a geometrically interpretable Lyapounov function, see chapter 1. The quotation is from Fisher, *Disequilibrium Foundations*, p. 26.

17. For a short survey of some of these models, see Hsieh and Mangum, *A Search for Synthesis*, chap. 11.

18. Alfred S. Eichner, "Introduction to the Symposium: Price Formation Theory," *Journal of Post Keynesian Economics 4*,1 (Fall 1981):82.

19. Shapiro and Nai-Pew Ong's articles are in *Journal of Post Keynesian Economics 4*,1 (Fall 1981):85–116. Josef Steindl, *Maturity and Stagnation in American Capitalism* (New York: Monthly Review Press, 1976).

20. See Mark H. Willes, "Rational Expectations as a Counterrevolution," in Daniel Bell and Irving Kristol, eds., *The Crisis in Economic Theory* (New York: Basic Books, 1981), pp. 85–90.

21. Rodney Maddock and Michael Carter, "A Child's Guide to Rational Expectations," *Journal of Economic Literature 20*, 1 (March 1982):49.

22. Paul Davies, *The Cosmic Blueprint* (New York: Simon & Schuster, 1988), p. 98.

23. Ibid.

24. Ivan Svitak, "The Source of Socialist Humanism," in Eric Fromm, ed., *Socialist Humanism: An International Symposium* (Garden City, NY: Doubleday, 1966), pp. 20–21.

25. Anthony Cutler, Barry Hindess, Paul Hirst, and Athar Hussain, *Marx's Capital and Capitalism Today*, 2 vols. (London: Routledge & Kegan Paul, 1977), p. 387.

26. Wesley Clair Mitchell, "Wesley Clair Mitchell on Veblen," in Henry William Spiegel, ed., *The Development of Economic Thought* (New York: John Wiley & Sons, 1952), p. 387.

27. Thorstein Veblen on Marx reprinted from Veblen's *The Place of Science in Modern Civilization* in Spiegel, ibid., p. 319.

28. Ben B. Seligman, *Main Currents in Modern Economics: Economic Thought since 1879* (New York: The Free Press of Glencoe, 1962), p. 157.

29. Philip Mirowski, *Against Mechanism: Protecting Economics from Science* (Totowa, NJ: Roman & Littlefield, 1988), p. 5.

30. Ibid., p. 115.

31. Ibid., p. 5. According to Mirowski, economics could be reconstructed from a hermeneutic perspective of a revised institutionalism. Such a reconstruction is not merely wishful thinking; there are signs that it is already well under way. In Mirowski's view, "economics needs protection from science, and especially from scientists such as Richard Feynman. Economics needs protection from the scientists in its midst. And worst of all, economics needs protection from itself. For years economics has enjoyed an impression of superiority over all other 'social sciences' in rigor, precision, and technical expertise" (p. 5).

32. Quoted by Fritjof Capra in *The Tao of Physics*, 2nd ed. (New York: Bantam Books, 1984), p. 4.

33. David Bohm, *Wholeness and the Implicate Order* (London: Ark Paperbacks, 1983), pp. 124–25.

34. Richard Feynman, *The Character of Physical Law* (Cambridge, MA:

MIT Press, 1989), p. 130. A detailed description of the two-slit experiment is given in chapter 6 of Feynman's book.

35. John Gribbin, *In Search of Schrodinger's Cat* (New York: Bantam Books, 1984), p. 172.

36. Davies, *The Cosmic Blueprint*, p. 23.

37. James Gleick, *Chaos: Making a New Science* (New York: Viking Penguin, 1987), p. 304.

38. Fritjof Capra, *The Turning Point* (New York: Bantam Books, 1983), pp. 413–14.

39. Ibid., p. 141.

40. Davies, *The Cosmic Blueprint*, pp. 198–99.

41. Paul Davies, *Other Worlds* (New York: Simon & Schuster, 1980), p. 74.

42. Capra, *The Turning Point*, p. 59.

43. Mirowski, *Against Mechanism*, p. 5.

44. Bruce Gregory, *Inventing Reality: Physics as Language* (New York: John Wiley, 1988), p. 183.

45. Ibid., p. 95.

46. Niels Bohr, quoted in Aage Paterson, "The Philosophy of Niels Bohr," in A. French and P. Kennedy, eds., *Niels Bohr: A Centenary Volume* (Cambridge, MA: Harvard University Press, 1985), p. 305.

47. Werner Heisenberg, *Physics and Philosophy*, (New York: Harper & Row, 1958), p. 58.

48. Gregory, *Inventing Reality*, p. 98.

49. Paul Davies, *Superforce: The Search for a Grand Unified Theory of Nature* (New York: Simon & Schuster, 1985), pp. 48–49.

50. Ibid., p. 49.

51. See the January/February 1990 issue of *Challenge*.

52. Amitai Etzioni, "A New Kind of Socioeconomics," *Challenge*, January/February 1990, p. 32.

53. Richard Swedberg, "The New 'Battle of Methods,' " *Challenge*, January/February 1990, p. 37.

54. Dugald Murdoch, *Niels Bohr's Philosophy of Physics* (Cambridge: Cambridge University Press, 1987), pp. 231–32.

55. Capra, *The Turning Point*, pp. 92–93.

56. Ibid., p. 94.

57. Martin Shubik, "A Curmudgeon's Guide to Microeconomics," *Journal of Economic Literature 8*, 2 (June 1970):406–7.

58. Alfred S. Eichner, ed., *A Guide to Post-Keynesian Economics* (Armonk, NY: M.E. Sharpe, 1978), p. 14.

59. Swedberg, "The New Battle of Methods," p. 36.

60. Ibid., p. 37. The term "economic imperialism" in Swedberg's words, refers to the approach that threatens to worsen the isolation of economics by increasing the traditional distrust among economists for sociologists, historians, and other scholars in the social sciences. It does this by its claim that neoclassical economics can solve all problems in the social sciences much better than the traditional approaches.

Bibliography

Aschheim, Joseph, and Ching-Yao Hsieh. *Macroeconomics: Income and Monetary Theory*. Washington, DC: University Press of America, 1980.

Atkins, K.R. *Physics*. New York: John Wiley, 1965.

Barnett, Lincoln. *The Universe and Dr. Einstein*. New York: Signet, New American Library, 1984.

Barone, E. "The Ministry of Production in the Collective State." In F.A. Hayek, ed., *Collective Economics Planning*. London: Routledge & Kegan Paul, 1935.

Barrow, John D., and Frank J. Tipler. *The Anthropic Cosmological Principle*. New York: Oxford University Press, 1986.

Baumol, William J., and Jess Benhabib. "Chaos: Significance, Mechanism, and Economic Applications." *Journal of Economic Perspectives 3*, 1 (Winter 1989):77–105.

Benessay, Jean-Pascal. *The Economics of Market Disequilibrium*. New York: Academic Press, 1982.

Blaug, Mark. *The Methodology of Economics: Or How Economists Explain*. Cambridge: Cambridge University Press, 1980.

Bleaney, Michael. *Underconsumption Theories: A History and Critical Analysis*. New York: International Publishers, 1976.

Bohm, David. *Quantum Theory*. Englewood Cliffs, NJ: Prentice-Hall, 1951.

———. *Unfolding Meaning*. London: Ark Paperbacks, 1987.

———. *Wholeness and the Implicate Order*. London: Ark Paperbacks, 1983.

Bohm, David, and B. Hiley. "On the Intuitive Understanding of Non-locality as Implied by Quantum Theory." *Foundations of Physics 5* (1975).

Bohr, Niels. *The Philosophical Writings of Niels Bohr*, vol. 1–3. Woodbridge, CT: Ox Bow Press, 1987. [A reprint of the original publication by Cambridge University Press, 1934].

Boland, Lawrence A. *The Foundation of Economic Method*. London: Allen & Unwin, 1982.

Boulding, Kenneth E. "The Economics of the Coming Spaceship Earth." In Herman E. Daly, ed., *Toward a Steady-State Economy*. San Francisco, W.H. Freeman, 1973.

———. "Economics as a Moral Science." In *Economics as a Science*. New York: McGraw-Hill, 1970.

Brinton, Crane. *The Shaping of Modern Thought*. Englewood Cliffs, NJ: Prentice-Hall, 1950.

Brock, William A. "Distinguishing Random and Deterministic Systems: Abridged Version." *Journal of Economic Theory 40* (1986).

Brock, W.A., and C.L. Sayers. "Is the Business Cycle Characterized by Deterministic Chaos?" *Journal of Monetary Economics 22* (1988).

Burmeister, Edwin, and A. Rodney Dobell. *Mathematical Theories of Economic Growth*. London: Macmillian, 1970.

Calder, Nigel. *Einstein's Universe*. New York: Viking Penguin, 1979.

Capaldi, Nicholas, ed. *The Enlightenment: The Proper Study of Mankind*. New York: Capricorn Books, 1968.

Capra, Fritjof. *The Tao of Physics*. New York: Bantam Books, 1977.

———. *The Turning Point*. New York: Bantam Books, 1983.

———. *Uncommon Wisdom: Conversations with Remarkable People*. New York: Simon & Schuster, 1988.

Chaisson, Eric. *Relatively Speaking: Relativity, Black Holes, and the Fate of the Universe*. New York: W.W. Norton, 1988.

Colpeston, Frederick C. *Medieval Philosophy*. New York: Harper & Row, 1961.

Commons, John R. *Institutional Economics*. Madison: University of Wisconsin Press, 1961.

Crutchfield, J.P., J.D. Farmer, N.H. Packard, and R.S. Shaw. "Chaos." *Scientific American*, December 1986.

Cutler, Anthony, Barry Hindess, Paul Hirst, and Athar Hussain. *Marx's Capital and Capitalism Today*, 2 vols. London: Routledge & Kegan Paul, 1977.

d'Abro, A. *The Evolution of Scientific Thought: From Newton to Einstein*, 2nd ed. New York: Dover Publications, 1950.

Dalton, George, ed. *Primitive, Archaic and Modern Economies: Essays of Karl Polanyi*. Garden City, NY: Doubleday, 1968.

Daly, Herman E. *Economics, Ecology, Ethics*. San Francisco: W.H. Freeman, 1980.

———, ed. *Toward a Steady-State Economy*. San Francisco: W.H. Freeman, 1973.

Davidson, Paul. *Money and the Real World*, 2nd ed. New York: John Wiley & Sons, 1978.

———. "Rational Expectations: A Fallacious Foundation for Studying Crucial Decision-Making Processes." *Journal of Post Keynesian Econmics 5*, 2 (Winter 1982–83).

Davies, Paul. *The Cosmic Blueprint*. New York: Simon & Schuster, 1988.

————. *Other Worlds*. New York: Simon & Schuster, 1980.

————. *Superforce: The Search for a Grand Unified Theory of Nature*. New York: Simon & Schuster, 1985.

Davis, Philip J., and Reuben Hersh. *The Mathematical Experience*. Boston: Houghton Mifflin, 1981.

Dewey, John. *The Quest for Certainty*. New York: G.P. Putnam's Sons, 1960.

Duncan, Graeme. *Marx and Mill*. Cambridge: Cambridge University Press, 1973.

Durant, Will. *The Story of Philosophy*. New York: Simon & Schuster, 1953.

Eddington, Arthur. *The Nature of the Physical World*. Ann Arbor: University of Michigan Press, 1958.

————. *New Pathways in Science*. Ann Arbor: University of Michigan Press, 1959.

Eichner, Alfred E. "Introduction to the Symposium: Price Formation Theory." *Journal of Post Keynesian Economics 4*, 1 (Fall 1981).

————, ed. *A Guide to Post-Keynesian Economics*. Armonk, NY: M.E. Sharpe, 1978.

Einstein, Albert. *Relativity: The Special and General Theory*, trans. by Robert W. Lawson. New York: Crown, 1916.

Etzioni, Amitai. "A Kind of Socioeconomics." *Challenge*, January/February 1990.

Ferguson, Charles E. *The Neoclassical Theory of Production and Distribution*. Cambridge: Cambridge University Press, 1969.

Feynman, Richard P. *The Character of Physical Law*. 15th ptg. Cambridge, MA: MIT Press, 1989.

————. *QED (Quantum Electrodynamics): The Strange Theory of Light and Matter*. Princeton, NJ: Princeton University Press, 1985.

Fisher, Franklin M. *Disequilibrium Foundations of Equilibrium Economics*. New York: Cambridge University Press, 1983.

French, A.P. *Special Relativity*. New York: W.W. Norton, 1968.

Fromm, Eric. *Escape from Freedom*. New York: Avon Books, 1941.

Gale, Douglas. *Money: In Disequilibrium*. Cambridge: University Press, 1983.

Gardner, Martin. *The Relativity Explosion*. New York: Vintage Books, 1976.

Georgescu-Roegen, Nicholas. "The Entropy Law and the Economic Problem." In Herman E. Daly, ed., *Economics, Biology, Ethics: Essays toward a Steady-State Economy*. San Francisco: W.H. Freeman, 1980.

————. *The Entropy Law and the Economic Process*. Cambridge, MA: Harvard University Press, 1971.

Gleick, James. *Chaos: Making a New Science*. New York: Viking, 1987.

Goldfarb, Robert S. "If (as M. Blaug, H. Johnson, W. Leontief, B. Ward and Others Have Claimed) Economists Do Not Severely Test Their Theories, What's All This Empirical Work in Economics about, Anyway?" Unpublished working paper, Department of Economics, George Washington University, 1989.

Goodwin, R.M. "The Non-linear Accelerator and the Persistence of Business Cycles." *Econometrica 19* (1951).

Grandmont, Jean-Michel. "On Endogenous Competitive Business Cycles." *Econometrica 53* (1985):995–1045.

Grandmont, Jean-Michel, and P. Malgrange. "Nonlinear Economic Dynamics: Introduction." *Journal of Economic Theory 40* (1986).

Gregory, Bruce. *Inventing Reality: Physics as Language.* New York: Bantam Books, 1984.

Gribbin, John. *In Search of Schrodinger's Cat.* New York: Bantam Books, 1984.

Hahn, Frank H. "On the Stability of Pure Exchange Equilibrium." *International Economic Review 3* (1962).

————. "A Stable Adjustment Process for a Competitive Economy." *Review of Economic Studies 29* (1962).

Hahn, Frank H., and T. Negishi. "A Theorem on Non-Tatonnement Stability." *Econometrica 30* (1962).

Hawking, Stephen W. *A Brief History of Time.* New York: Bantam Books, 1988.

Heilbroner, Robert L. *The Future as History.* New York: Grove Press, 1959.

Heisenberg, Werner. *Philosophic Problems of Nuclear Science.* Greenwich, CT: Fawcett Publications, 1952.

————. *Physics and Philosophy.* New York: Harper & Row, 1958.

Henderson, Hazel. *Creating Alternative Futures.* New York: Putnam, 1978.

Hey, John D. *Economics in Disequilibrium.* Cambridge: Cambridge University Press, 1983.

————. *Uncertainty in Microeconomics.* New York: New York University Press, 1979.

Hicks, John. *Causality in Economics.* New York: Basic Books, 1979.

————. *A Contribution to the Theory of the Trade Cycle.* New York: Oxford University Press, 1950.

————. *Value and Capital.* Oxford: Oxford University Press, 1939.

Hsieh, Ching-Yao et al. *A Short Introduction to Modern Growth Theory.* Washington, D.C.: University Press of America, 1978.

Hsieh, C.Y., and Stephen L. Mangum. *A Search for Synthesis in Economic Theory.* Armonk, NY: M.E. Sharpe, 1986.

Intriligator, Michael E. *Mathematical Optimization and Economic Theory.* Englewood Cliffs, NJ: Prentice-Hall, 1971.

Jantsch, Eric. *The Self-Organizing Universe.* Oxford: Pergamon Press, 1980.

Jeans, James. *Physics and Philosophy.* Ann Arbor: University of Michigan Press, 1966. [First published by the Cambridge University Press.]

Kaku, Michio, and Jennifer Trainer. *Beyond Einstein: The Cosmic Quest for the Theory of the Universe.* New York: Bantam Books, 1987.

Katouzian, Homa. *Ideology and Method in Economics.* New York: New York University Press, 1980.

Kauder, Emil. *A History of Marginal Utility Theory.* Princeton, NJ: Princeton University Press, 1965.

Keynes, John Maynard. *The General Theory of Employment, Interest and Money.* London: Macmillan, 1951.

Kirzner, Israel. "On the Method of Austrian Economics." In Edwin G. Dolan, ed., *The Foundations of Modern Austrian Economics*. Kansas City, MO: Sheed & Ward, 1976.

Kline, Morris. *Mathematics in Western Culture*. New York: Oxford University Press, 1964.

Kolakowski, Leszek. *The Alienation of Reason: A History of Positivist Thought*. New York: Doubleday, 1969.

Kuhn, Thomas S. *The Copernican Revolution*. New York: Vintage Books, 1957.

————. *The Structure of Scientific Revolutions*, 2nd enl. ed. Chicago: University of Chicago Press, 1970.

Lange, O., and F. Taylor. *On the Economic Theory of Socialism*. Minneapolis: University of Minnesota Press, 1938.

Lavine, T.Z. *From Socrates to Sartre: The Philosophic Quest*. New York: Bantam Books, 1984.

Maddock, Rodney, and Michael Carter. "A Child's Guide to Rational Expectations." *Journal of Economic Literature 20*, 1 (March 1982).

Mandelbrot, B.B. *The Fractal Geometry of Nature*. San Francisco: W.H. Freeman, 1982.

————. "The Variation of Certain Speculative Prices." *Journal of Business* 36 (1963):394–419.

Margenau, Henry. "Einstein's Conception of Reality." in Paul Arthur Schilpp, ed., *Albert Einstein: Philosopher-Scientist*. New York: Harper & Row.

Marshall, Alfred. *Principles of Economics*, 8th ed. New York: Macmillan, 1953.

Marx, Karl, and Friedrich Engels. *Manifesto of the Communist Party*. In Marx and Engels, *Basic Writings on Politics and Philosophy*, ed. by Lewis S. Feuer. Garden City, NY: Anchor Books, 1959.

Meadows, Donella H., Dennis L. Meadows, Jorgen Randers, and William W. Behrens III. *The Limits to Growth*. New York: Universe Books, 1972.

Mill, John Stuart. *Principles of Political Economy with Some of Their Applications to Social Philosophy*, vols. 1 & 2. London: John W. Parker and Son, 1957.

Mini, Piero V. *Philosophy and Economics*. Gainesville: University Press of Florida, 1974.

Mirowski, Philip. *Against Mechanism*. Totowa, NJ: Roman & Littlefield, 1988.

Mishan, E.J. "The Growth of Affluence and the Decline of Welfare." In Herman E. Daly, ed. *Economics, Ecology, Ethics*. San Francisco: W.H. Freeman, 1980.

Mitchell, Wesley Clair. "Westly Clair Mitchell on Veblen." In Henry W. Spiegel, ed., *The Development of Economic Thought*. New York: John Wiley, 1952.

Murdoch, Dugald. *Niels Bohr's Philosophy of Physics*. Cambridge: Cambridge University Press, 1987.

Myrdal, Gunnar. *The Political Element in the Development of Economic Theory*. New York: Simon & Schuster, 1954.

Northrop, F.S.C. "Introduction." In Werner Heisenberg, *Physics and Philosophy*. New York: Harper & Row, 1958.

O'Driscoll, G.P., Jr., and M.J. Rizzo, with a contribution by R.W. Garrison. *The Economics of Time and Ignorance*. New York: Basil Blackwell, 1985.

Okie, Susan. "The Disposable Society's 16 Billion-Diaper Question." *The Washington Post*, January 8, 1990.

Ortega y Gasset, José. *The Revolt of the Masses*. New York: W.W. Norton, 1932.

Paterson, Aage. "The Philosophy of Niels Bohr." In A. French and P. Kennedy, eds., *Niels Bohr: A Centenary Volume*. Cambridge, MA: Harvard University Press, 1985.

Patinkin, Don. *Money, Interest, and Prices*. 2nd ed. New York: Harper & Row, 1965.

Peitgen, H.O., and P.H. Richter. *The Beauty of Fractals*. Berlin: Springer-Verlag, 1986.

Planck, Max. *The Philosophy of Physics*. New York: W.W. Norton, 1936.

Popper, Karl, and John Eccles. *The Self and Its Brain*. Berlin: Springer International, 1977.

Prigogine, Ilya, and Isabelle Stengers. *Order out of Chaos*. New York: Bantam Books, 1984.

Reichenbach, Hans. "The Philosophical Significance of the Theory of Relatively." In Paul Arthur Schilpp, ed., *Albert Einstein: Philosopher-Scientist*. New York: Harper & Row, 1959.

Robinson, Joan. *Economic Philosophy*. Chicago: Aldine, 1962.

———. "Solow on the Rate of Return." In *Collected Economic Papers*, vol. 3. Oxford: Blackwell, 1965.

Rothbard, Murray N. "The Mantel of Science." In Helmut Schoek and James W. Wiggins, eds., *Scientism and Values*. Princeton, NJ: D. Van Nostrand Co., 1960.

Routh, Guy. "Economics and Chaos." *Challenge*, July/August 1989.

Russell, Bertrand. *The ABC of Relativity*. London: Allen & Unwin, 1958.

———. *A History of Western Philosophy*. New York: Simon & Schuster, 1945.

Samuelson, Paul A. *Foundations of Economic Analysis*. Cambridge, MA: Harvard University Press, 1958.

Schenk, H.G. *The Mind of the European Romantics*. Garden City, NY: Doubleday, 1969.

Schumacher, E.F. "The Age of Plenty: A Christian View." In Daly, *Economics, Ecology, Ethics*.

———. "Buddhist Economics." Resurgence 1 (January–February 1968). Reprinted in Daly, *Economics, Ecology, Ethics*.

———. *Small is Beautiful: Economics as if People Mattered*. New York: Harper & Row, 1973.

Schumpeter, Joseph A. *History of Western Philosophy*. New York: Oxford University Press, 1954.

Seligman, Ben B. *Main Currents in Modern Economics: Economic Thought since 1870*. New York: The Free Press of Glencoe, 1962.

Shapiro, Nina. "Pricing and The Growth of the Firm." *Journal of Post Keynesian Economics 4*, 1 (Fall 1981).

Sheldrake, Rupert. *New Science of Life*. Los Angeles: J.P. Tarcher, 1981.

Shubik, Martin. "A Curmudgeon's Guide to Microeconomics." *Journal of Economic Literature 8*, 2 (June 1970):406–7.

Spengler, Oswald. *The Decline of the West*, vol. 1, trans. by Charles Francis Atkinson. New York: Alfred A. Knopf, 1926.

Stanlis, Peter J. *Edmund Burke and the Natural Law*. Ann Arbor: University of Michigan Press, 1965.

Steindl, Josef. *Maturity and Stagnation in American Capitalism*. New York: Monthly Review Press, 1976.

Svitak, Ivan. "The Source of Socialist Humanism." In Erich Fromm, ed., *Socialist Humanism: An International Symposium*. Garden City, NY: Anchor Books, 1966.

Swedberg, Richard. "The New 'Battle of Methods.'" *Challenge*, January/February 1990.

Tawney, Richard H. *Religion and the Rise of Capitalism*. New York: New American Library, 1947.

Taylor Edward F., and John A. Wheeler. *Spacetime Physics*. New York: W.H. Freeman, 1966.

Uzawa, H. "The Stability of Dynamic Process." *Econometrica 29* (1961): 317–31.

———. "On the Stability of Edgeworth's Barter Process." *International Economic Review 3* (1962):218–82.

Viner, Jacob. *Studies in the Theory of International Trade*. New York: Harper & Row, 1937.

Ward, Benjamin. *What's Wrong with Economics?* New York: Basic Books, 1972.

Weintraub, E. Roy. *Micro-Foundations*. London: Cambridge University Press, 1979.

Weisskopf, Walter A. *The Psychology of Economics*. Chicago: University of Chicago Press, 1955.

Wible, James R. "Rational Expectations Tautologies." *Journal of Post Keynesian Economics 5*, 2 (Winter 1982–83):199–203.

Willes, Mark H. "Rational Expectations as a Counterrevolution." In Daniel Bell and Irving Kristol, eds., *The Crisis in Economic Theory*. New York: Basic Books, 1981.

Wilshire, Bruce, ed. *Romanticism and Revolution: The Nineteenth Century*. New York: Capricorn Books, 1968.

Wolf, Fred Alan. *Taking the Quantum Leap*. San Francisco: Harper & Row, 1981.

Worland, Stephen Theodore. *Scholasticism and Welfare Economics*. Notre Dame: University of Notre Dame Press, 1967.

Index

About the Authors

Ching-Yao Hsieh received his graduate degrees in economics at George Washington University, where he taught for twenty-seven years and is now Professor Emeritus. Before joining the university, he served as Alternate Executive Director for China at the International Monetary Fund from 1955 to 1959. He is co-author of *Macroeconomics: Income and Monetary Theory* (1967), and author of *A Short Introduction to Modern Growth Theory* (1978) and *A Search for Synthesis in Economic Theory* (1986). He has also lectured at the Industrial College of the Armed Forces and at the Foreign Service Institute of the Department of State.

Meng-Hua Ye is currently Assistant Professor of Economics at George Washington University, after receiving his Ph.D. in Economics at the University of Wisconsin-Madison.